The Belinda Chronicles

Praise for *The Belinda Chronicles*

The Belinda Chronicles expertly illuminates aspects of the human condition that connect us all. Seidel's beautifully rendered vignettes on family and aging are rich and resonant, unflinching and honest. A true pleasure to read. — **Laura McHugh, award-winning author of** *The Weight of Blood*

*****

Genealogy as a tender story of coming to terms with self-identity later in life. Using memory, imagination, and evidence, Seidel builds a candid, but always respectful, narrative based on her elders. The voice is at once wry, sad, funny, and joyful. — **Elizabeth Klaver, author of** *Sites of Autopsy* **and editor of** *The Body in Medical Culture*

*****

Linda Seidel is sweet, caustic, funny, smart. Like her savvy characters, she doesn't flinch in her observations of death's presence. Life at the end may be "a disappointing business," to paraphrase a character in *The Belinda Chronicles,* but there are nevertheless "moments of delight." Witness them here in this lovely honoring, warm and gritty, all the stuff of family. — **Jocelyn Cullity, author of** *Amah & the Silk-Winged Pigeons* **and** *The Envy of Paradise*

*****

The Belinda Chronicles invites readers to enter the quietly brewing, fertile headspace of small-town feminist icon, Belinda, whose advancing age serves to illuminate rather than diminish her agency. With wry humor, candor and empathy, Linda Seidel offers aptly titled, pithy portraits of her characters in the throes of dementia, marriage, infidelity, physical frailty, and delight. These brief-but-deep dives into the quiet spaces of human behavior intertwine in a complex network of textured familial relationships. Central to the book's power is Belinda's expanding self-awareness. Ruminating on her youthful appearance in "The Ingenue," Belinda cuts through vanity and ambivalence to make this pointed reflection: "She wondered whether she wants to be taken seriously. Maybe it was a source of freedom not to be." Complex truths are sprinkled throughout Seidel's concise chronicles, giving the reader little to read, and much to ponder. Belinda's journey may seem to be a deliberate coming to terms with death, but upon reflection, in the words of Belinda, hers is a satisfyingly "edgy tale" of coming to terms with life. —- **Becky Becker, Professor of Theatre at Clemson University, writer, director, and recent editor for** *Theatre Symposium: A Journal of the Southeastern Theatre Conference*

*****

A work of austere tenderness and the most serious kind of playfulness. Seidel's fearless mindwalk confronts durable philosophical paradoxes of memory, reality and its construction, and the unity of personality and its ephemerality — without ever losing the plain, important narrative of about-to-turn-70 Belinda, blinking into deep time and trying to figure out what it adds up to.

Deeply aware of what [time] did to her parents' faculties, Seidel's narrator has a consciousness aware of its own self-construction, made urgent by knowledge of its inevitable dissolution.

The narrator, an admirably self-sufficient woman, remembers her way through her ancestral lines, trying, essentially, to grasp how she got here, and what here-ness amounts to once one's gone. Repeatedly she tries to fill in the space between the actual self of a person who once was, and the image etched in her own memory. A person of intellectual and moral courage, she tells herself and her readers no lies about just how unsettling the inquiry is. Both haunting and triumphant. — **Adam Davis, professor of English at Truman State University, webmaster for the Missouri Folklore Society, and managing editor for** *Green Hills Literary Lantern*

The Belinda Chronicles

by

Linda Seidel

Golden Antelope Press
715 E. McPherson
Kirksville, Missouri 63501
2020

ISBN: 978-1-952232-51-0

Library of Congress Control Number: 2020948349

Published by:
Golden Antelope Press
715 E. McPherson
Kirksville, Missouri 63501

Available at:
Golden Antelope Press
715 E. McPherson
Kirksville, Missouri, 63501
Phone: (660) 665-0273
http://www.goldenantelope.com
Email: ndelmoni@gmail.com

In memory of my elders

Note to the Reader

Many of the events in the following stories actually happened–or should have happened because they have become part of family lore. Nonetheless, I have changed most of the characters' names in order to give myself the freedom to invent detail, dialogue, and interpretations that are, at least partly, my own.

Contents

The Belinda Chronicles

Prologue: Belinda's Search for a Genre

Belinda was nearly 70. Maybe that's why she had the panicky feeling that she should be writing her memoirs, recording at least some of the details of her uneventful life so that if stroke or Alzheimer's wiped out her mind, she could still be said to have lived. Not that she had much faith in such an undertaking. "It would all be lies," she said to herself; "I've always told myself whatever I wanted to hear."

Besides, there was the problem of her name, Belinda, which she regarded as suitable, perhaps, for a child, but surely not for an elderly person already anticipating senility and death. She had never even met a Belinda except in the pages of *The Rape of the Lock*, and she had never much cared for the poetry of Alexander Pope. She considered that the forcible cutting of a young woman's hair, these days, would be considered as something like sexual harassment at the least, the perpetrator of which should have a restraining order taken out against him, rather than be celebrated in rhyming couplets.

Well, never mind her name. She would begin, setting down what she could remember or feel or predict, foment a crisis even, rather than retreat back into the pale gray vacuum where there was no story. And yet, she still had a problem: Belinda did not have a plot. Plots created suspense, imposed order on the chaos of random life events, and promised a recognizable conclusion that readers could anticipate. Even memoirs now required plots, especially those written by the ordinary person whose achievements were not intrinsically fascinating or whose friends were not famous. She needed that organizing principle that would drive her narrative forward, and she reviewed the tried-and-true formulas to which so many other writers had resorted. There was romantic comedy, for example, but she believed she was too old to star in one. Even in her younger days, she had never possessed the feminine charms to attract a Mr. Darcy. She was not only plain, but she was difficult, and she did not regret it. The brief years of her married life now seemed like a mirage.

The mystery genre seemed even less likely, even though it, too, had become a possibility for memoir writers who imagined that they could (like detectives) uncover essential truths of their lives. But the mystery plot depended on a smart, observant protagonist making sense of her surroundings, and Belinda knew that she lived too much inside her own head for this role. She had often berated herself for not seeing things taking place right in front of her own near-sighted eyes because those eyes were too often turned inward. No, the mystery plot would not do.

Belinda had always thought longingly of the coming-of-age plot, in which a young person reaches that point where she can launch herself into the world, achieving a new adult maturity as the result of transformative experience. The typical protagonist of this plot, of course, was the ingenue "waiting for life to start" (the girl described by Oscar Hammerstein in "Sixteen, Going on Seventeen"), like Elizabeth Bennet or Jane Eyre (the fictional Jane even claiming to write her own autobiography). But why couldn't that protagonist be an older person—someone who was already an adult but still had some things to learn?

In theory, the story of development for the aging person—in which the old person reaches a new insight or way of life, rather than simply dwindling into dementia or physical decrepitude—could be written, remained to be written, but depended upon creating a protagonist who could actually learn something. Was Belinda that person? Could she imagine a version of herself that could learn something? She was not sure. She feared she was more like one of those hapless Woody Allen characters who screwed up everything, pretended to gain new wisdom by the end, but most likely would continue to screw up everything.

Where would she look for that new wisdom anyway?

She began to think about the stories her family members had told her as a kind of legacy, the only wealth that she would ever receive from them, but enough. She began to think of the bittersweet scenes she had witnessed in the nursing home, where her parents had died painfully protracted deaths, as a kind of material to be sorted out and mined. She thought of the searing conflicts with her mother Trudi, never resolved in Trudi's lifetime, as writing problems to be tamed by a calm analysis of point of view. She realized that she had missed her chance with Trudi by not thinking in this way sooner. But she also recognized that the presence of the living woman—and the living conflict they shared—had unnerved her so that she lacked the empathetic perspective to get inside her mother's feelings while she was still alive. Maybe it was easier to understand the dead because they were not around to yell at you and elevate your blood pressure.

But neither were they around to act as a buffer against the world, to make Belinda, now an older person herself, feel safe. The world was not safe. It was not fair or just. Belinda had no protection against it except a comic sensibility and a self-ironizing view that would not allow her to become a merely self-deluded figure.

Part I

Women and Mothers

Memorial Day

Memorial Day was coming up, and Belinda had yet to buy flowers for her mother Trudi's grave. Trudi wasn't supposed to be buried in Middleville, Missouri, at all, but next to her second husband, Harry, back in Pennsylvania. Somehow, though, Belinda couldn't bring herself to do it: take her back there and stage a funeral among a group of virtual strangers. So, while Trudi lay wasting away in the nursing home, Belinda bought a plot—well, two plots actually: there was Leonard, her father, to think of—in the charming Middleville cemetery that dated back to the nineteenth century and featured tombstones of all sizes, shapes, and levels of grandiosity.

Belinda didn't know whether Trudi would approve and didn't ask her. Somehow Trudi seemed to have forgotten all about her second husband in the last few months when she had been so ill, and she was seeking a home in heaven, not in the ground, in any case.

Still, Belinda had long imagined taking a lawn chair out to the cemetery when the good weather came and arguing with Trudi's spirit. "Why am I here?" the ghost would say. "You never asked me whether you could cremate me or bury me in this godforsaken place. I miss Pennsylvania. How could I end up in here?" "But, Mom," Belinda would protest, "this is where I live. I never go to Pennsylvania any more. Who would visit you?"

But this little vision of ghostly communion ended on the day of the graveside ceremony about a month after Trudi died and the few interested relatives could be assembled. When the funeral director gave Belinda the urn with Trudi's ashes to place in the ground, Belinda knew that this was just a jar of leavings that had little to do with Trudi. No spirit hovered nearby. Belinda did not feel closer to Trudi in the cemetery than in any other place. The tombstone was

5

pretty, worth looking at once in a while. That was all.

Still, it was going to be Memorial Day. The flowers were to memo-rialize the person, to say to others, "This person is remembered." No reluctant ghost would upbraid Belinda. Perhaps Trudi would have done that job a few years back could she have anticipated Belinda's perfidy. But maybe not. Maybe the place of burial was just not that important. Rather, it was the life-and-death struggle to leave this earth that had animated Trudi's final passion and her frustration with a daughter who could not let her go.

Trudi's Parents

The wedding portrait

Recently retrieved from a pile of old family artifacts in a plastic box shoved under Belinda's bed, the small picture, newly framed, sits on the piano, itself a family heirloom rather than an instrument to be played.

The young woman in the photograph is not quite pretty, but is pleasing to behold. Her complexion is perfect, her waist is tiny, and she is deliciously petite. It is her wedding day, and she looks as good as she ever would, her body not yet thickened by child-bearing and debilitating hard work. She has flowers in her hair and a bouquet in her right hand, the left being tucked into the crook of her new husband's arm. Her gown is ornate and modest, covering every inch of her except her face and hands. She might have sewn it herself; she would have known how.

The young man is handsome, with his high forehead, deep-set eyes, and perfect mustache. He is taller than his wife. (His daughter Trudi would inherit his good looks, if not his stature.) His right arm, bent so that Lotte might grasp it, appears unnaturally rigid, his thumb protruding like a claw. Both Lotte and Fritz Bauer have the somber look of people in old photos who have been asked to hold their pose for too long.

Belinda does not know the date of the picture: 1910 or 1911, she would guess, given that the first baby came in 1912. The images in it fill her with questions. Was Lotte madly in love with her handsome man? Did she imagine that the worst times in her life were already behind her? She had survived the smallpox visitation on her family, when all the younger children died—six of her siblings according to

7

family lore—and only the two eldest and the parents recovered. What could be worse than that? And, in truth, Lotte would be fortunate in her offspring, who would all survive, prosper, and have children of their own. She would become the matriarch of a thriving family.

It was Fritz who would be lost to her, first during the war, the birthdates of her children telling the story: babies came in 1912, 1913, and 1914, and then there was a gap until Trudi was born in 1919. Even worse than the war gap was the fact that the man who came back to Lotte afterwards was not himself, not the boy she knew, and she urged him to apply for the government pension available to veterans who had been disabled in any way. Stubbornly, he refused. They would make a fresh start in America, he said; he would be all right. He would go on ahead. She would follow, only to find a man who no longer wanted his family.

Belinda wondered where Lotte had found Fritz in the first place. Trudi had suggested that he may have been a hand on the family farm. Did Lotte find his good looks irresistible? Did he find her strength and industry attractive? Belinda could not help but attribute agency to her grandmother, the woman she knew, rather than to the shadowy grandfather who would always remain a mystery.

The orphanage

Trudi must have been nine or ten years old when her parents' fight one evening was loud enough to cause the neighbors to call the cops. It was, maybe, 1929 or 1930, and the family had lived in Brewer, Pennsylvania, for about five years. Trudi's mother Lotte hardly ever got angry when Fritz beat her; she just looked sad. Afterwards, she would tell Trudi, "Your father has never been 'right'" (in his mind) "since the war." Lotte meant the big war in Europe when Fritz had fought for Germany and worn one of those helmets with a spike on top. Trudi had seen pictures.

But on the night in question, Fritz was brandishing the carving knife from the kitchen, and Lotte knew that she had to save herself, so she screamed bloody murder. By the time the cops came and arrested him, Fritz was sobbing remorsefully, but Lotte didn't stop them from taking him to jail. She knew that her life was at stake, and she thought that if he killed her, there would be no one to take care of the kids. The older ones were almost grown up, but Trudi was a little girl still and small for her age. Besides, Lotte didn't know that Fritz would never come home again: he would be evaluated by a doctor and sent to the state mental institution a few miles away. Even more humiliating, maybe, was the fact that the authorities saw fit to put her kids in an orphanage for a few weeks until the home situation "stabilized," as they put it. What sort of mother had her kids stolen from her?

Trudi forgot most of this not long after it happened. You might say that she actively suppressed these memories. She belonged to a poor but respectable family, and respectable people didn't get kidnapped out of their houses and sent to an orphanage. It never happened.

But then one night, many years later, when her own life was almost over, she had a dream. In the dream, she was crying as if her heart would break. She was lying on a smelly mattress, the old urine left by some other miserable child visible beneath the thin sheet. She was in the little girls' dormitory; her sisters were older and slept in a separate place. How she wanted them!

"What's wrong, Trudi?" a kindly nun asked. "Do you need to go to the outhouse? I could walk you there."

"Yes," said Trudi. There was no point in trying to explain what was really wrong. She didn't know if she could explain it anyway.

The dream ended when she woke with a jolt as some busy aide opened the drapes of her nursing home room to let in the early morning sunlight. "This is just as bad as being in the orphanage," thought Trudi; "at least I got out of the orphanage." And then she remembered: it wasn't just a dream; it was a memory. She had really been in an orphanage. Well, she wouldn't tell Belinda. That girl's head was always in the clouds. She'd tell the other one when she came to visit. Her name might be Delores. She listened better.

Lotte

"My parents had a farm once, back in Germany, but it was lost in the war," began Lotte. It was a family party, and people were moving in and out of the room. No one was paying attention to the story Lotte wanted to tell. Belinda didn't even bother to say, "That's too bad, Nana." Old people's memories were about ancient history, not something you had to pay attention to now.

Lotte subsided. She didn't mind that her spoiled grandchildren would always think of her as some dirt-poor peasant living in a hut with an earthen floor in the old country. That is the state to which she and Fritz and their children had been reduced. But there had been an earlier time when her parents had been prosperous farmers before hard-fought battles rendered so much East Prussian landscape unrecognizable and so many farmers irrecoverably destroyed. War wasn't just about winning and losing, or soldiers who would never be the same again. It also took away people's homes and their place in the world. There had been no reason not to emigrate to Brewer, Pennsylvania, if that is what Fritz wanted to do.

Fritz went first. The plan was for him to establish himself in some decent job and then to send for her and the children. But, somehow, he never earned enough money to send her any for their passage. Lotte knew she would have to act; she borrowed money from her cousin in Brewer, promising to pay him back on the installment plan. She had no doubt she could do this. Brewer, from what she had heard, was a bustling industrial city, and she was a talented seamstress, her parents having sent her to Warsaw when she was still a girl specifically to acquire this skill. She would always be able to find work. Later, she would wonder whether her younger descendants had any conception of how hard she had worked for the family to which they

10

all belonged. She thought not.

She had raised four children almost by herself, and they had all prospered, married, and had children of their own. She had done her job well under circumstances that had seemed impossible at times, although no one seemed to remember that now. Now she was just a useless old woman who didn't speak English very well, but God knew what she had done. No one could take that away.

It is true that Belinda had long been hazily aware that Lotte's life had not been easy—that she had had to function as a single mother for most of her life as a parent; that none of the three languages (German, Polish, and Russian) in which Lotte was already fluent were much help to her when she arrived in Brewer at the age of 40 and had to learn English; that she had been abused at home and probably exploited at work. But none of these circumstances made much of an impression upon Belinda. She could have regarded the old lady as a woman of the world, a survivor, a heroine, but she did not. When she looked at Lotte, she saw an unfashionable old woman from a place that didn't even exist anymore, and that was all.

Maybe one of the many reasons she felt distant from her German grandmother was that Belinda had never understood any deeply religious person. It's true that Belinda had been subjected to the usual forms of Lutheran indoctrination: Sunday school and confirmation class; and she did try for a while to adhere to the expected party line, but to the literal-minded child, the dogma made no sense. The Trinity was obviously a logical absurdity. (She thought she might have persisted with religious belief a little longer had she been allowed to become a Unitarian, but Leonard looked at the relevant pamphlets she was reading as if they were Communist propaganda and so she threw them all away.) Later it became clear to her that heaven and hell were fantasies and that there was no personal god who would listen to your prayers, although the impersonal god of the deists (the force that set the whole universe in motion) still seemed a possibility.

Belinda understood that conventional religious belief met important communal needs. People liked to gather together to hear sacred messages and do important work—or, alternatively, to show off their new clothes. These things were not mutually exclusive. Then there were the dangers of everyday life against which a quick prayer could offer reassurance. Belinda could not enumerate the times when conventional believers explained to her that God had personally in-

tervened in their lives to prevent a major car crash when they had
summoned His assistance. "What about all the people who die in
wrecks? Didn't they say the right prayer?" she would counter irrev-
erently. (Belinda, who knew she was a bad driver, drove as little as
possible, since she had no god to protect her.)

Her grandmother Lotte, though, would not have appealed to her
God, thought Belinda, in such a crass, instrumentalist way. Lotte was
the real thing, a woman of faith who might allow her spirit to be
soothed by the golden words of Billy Graham (an advisor to presi-
dents, after all), but who didn't need anyone in her later years to tell
her what to believe. Her life had been a trial by fire, and she couldn't
say that she had come through unscathed, but she felt that she had
prevailed.

Later, Belinda would remember the last time she saw Lotte with
some regret. It was Aunt Frieda's Christmas Eve party in 1975. Belinda was 26; Lotte was 90. "I hope you have a good life," Lotte said
earnestly to her granddaughter, who was nonplussed, then dismis-
sive. "Oh, but I'll see you again," she said and escaped out the door.
"She's still a thoughtless child," said Lotte to herself, but she really
did wish Belinda well, because the girl was her own flesh and blood,
and life was hard.

Death of Helen

When Ladue tried to wake Helen at 6:30 am (in time for the 7:30 breakfast), she found the old woman unrousable. She called Helen's name loudly and tried to find a pulse, but clearly Helen was gone. She had died in her sleep some time after the 4:00 am check. It was the perfect death, really, thought Ladue, who nonetheless wished it had not happened on this particular day, Ladue's birthday, which was reminder enough of her own mortality.

Soon everyone in the nursing home became aware of Helen's passing, and several people accosted Belinda with the news when she arrived to feed Leonard his lunch. Belinda started crying immediately—the tears she had not shed for Trudi two months before, the tears that really were for Trudi. She dabbed at her eyes surreptitiously, and commiserated with Ladue that her birthday had been spoiled.

Helen had been Trudi's quiet, introverted roommate, a harmless old lady who liked to read when her physical condition allowed her to do so. Belinda could weep for her easily because she had nothing to regret or feel guilty for. Her slight acquaintance with Helen was not fraught with ambivalence. Besides, there were Belinda's irrational fears that if only she had done X, Y, or Z, Trudi, who was 98 at the time of her death, would still be alive. There was no power struggle between Belinda and Helen, who was just a nice old lady.

Belinda had to remind herself that that is how most people had seen Trudi—as just a nice old lady—not a person with whom one could possibly be locked in a contest of wills.

Trudi Feels Oppressed

"Time for physical therapy," said the red-haired girl cheerfully. Trudi was aware that the red-haired girl was a professional physical therapist in her late 30's, but that still made her a girl to a woman of 98. For that matter, the well-intentioned but tiresome Belinda was also still a girl in Trudi's book.

"But I thought I was done with physical therapy," Trudi managed to get out. Speech was difficult for her—had been so ever since the series of small strokes she had had twenty-some years before, leaving her ability to walk and talk sadly diminished.

"Oh, your six weeks were over last week," admitted Jess, "but then your daughter begged that you be allowed to continue since you seem to like it so much."

Trudi looked outraged, thinking but not saying that Belinda had never asked her whether she wanted more physical therapy. Trudi understood that Belinda still had some sort of fantasy that she could be restored to her previous tenuous state of health before a series of illnesses had laid her low for the past nine months—a sort of gestation, not of life, but of death.

"Look, Trudi, you don't have to do PT if you don't want to. It's entirely up to you," said Jess.

"I'll do it," said Trudi, and, really, she was proud of her performance that day, anger giving her a temporary zest that she could not conceal. But she thought that she would tell off Belinda. It was bad enough that her husbands, first Leonard and then Harry, had told her what to do, so that marriage had become an exercise in self-suppression. Now this girl, her own daughter, was treating her in the same way. It was too much.

The next day Trudi was enjoying a morning in bed when her fa-

14

vorite aide, Darlene, came in and announced that it was time to get up and eat lunch. "Oh, let me be, I'm sleeping," complained Trudi without anger.

"You know I love you, Sugar," said Darlene, kissing Trudi on the forehead, "but you need to get up and eat something."

Trudi was thinking this over when Belinda walked in. "Oh, Mom, you should do what Darlene says. Then we could have lunch and pretty soon you'll be strong enough for outings to the lake again." There was an edge of hysteria to her speech.

Darlene was dismayed. Now she'd have to go and get another aide and force Trudi to get up. She sighed. She could see that Belinda had no clue that she had just made everything more difficult. But soon Trudi was dressed, in her wheelchair, sitting at her accustomed lunch table, waiting for her food to come. Belinda sat with her.

Trudi waited until there were no extraneous people hovering nearby. Then she looked directly at Belinda and spat out, "I wish you would die!"

Trudi saw the stricken look of hurt and rage on Belinda's face, and she might have relented at that very moment, had not Belinda begun to laugh. "Everyone dies, Mom, so I'm sure you'll get your wish," Belinda chuckled nastily, wondering when Trudi had turned into such a bitch.

Trudi in the Hospital

"Have you given up?" Belinda asked Trudi, who was lying in bed in the Middleville Hospital one evening a few weeks later. She was recovering from pneumonia and a urinary tract infection, making good progress despite the fact that she had eaten almost nothing in the five days she had been hospitalized. One of Trudi's doctors had lectured Belinda, "We can cure infection here, but your mother will get one after another if she doesn't start eating better."

Eating, then, was a life-or-death business. Everyone knew that. Somehow Belinda imagined that it was her job to get Trudi to eat, that Trudi's doctor had given her this mandate. Later, much later, Belinda would interpret the doctor's words differently—that he had been gently trying to tell her that Trudi was dying.

Still, five days of starvation constituted a statement that penetrated, if only briefly, even Belinda's wall of denial. And so she had to ask, "Have you given up?" Trudi said yes, tears leaking slowly from her eyes. "I loved my mother," said Trudi, "but not like you love me."

Belinda did not understand. Was this a reversal of the nasty comment Trudi had launched at her three weeks before? Belinda knew for a fact that she was not especially loving in the only way that counted: making the other person *feel* loved. So what did Trudi mean? Eventually, but not in Trudi's lifetime, Belinda came to understand that Trudi had been telling her again, telling her more kindly, "Please let me go. Your work here is over."

16

Marty the Nurse

Marty had been a nurse for 20 years, but the nursing home was a new beat for her, and she was not entirely happy with what she saw. The old people—the residents—were mostly pretty stoic. She had no quarrel with them. But the family members were something else again.

Take the old woman Trudi, for example, who had just come back from the hospital a few days before. Marty would never have sent her there to begin with: it was just prolonging the agony of a clearly dying woman, who had tolerated the Lucky Stroke nursing home for four years and clearly had had enough. But her daughter Belinda was convinced that Trudi was having one more miraculous recovery, eating again, at least in front of her daughter, and winning praise for her progress in physical therapy. Of course, Belinda did not see Trudi spit out her pills or refuse food more often than she took it. Trudi had told Marty flat out that she was done with this world; she was ready to go. Yes, she did the physical therapy: it was the one time she could move her body and feel her remaining strength. She wouldn't have anyone say she died because she was too weak to continue.

"Oh, that woman is a pistol," thought Marty; "too bad her daughter doesn't see it." She had to admit, though, that Darlene was almost as bad, worshipping Trudi as if she were a princess. One morning Darlene was trying to feed Trudi her lunch, while the old lady shook her head and pushed away the bowls of pureed food in front of her. "You know what will happen if you don't eat, don't you, Sugar?" purred Darlene. Marty saw a flash of lightning cross Trudi's face before she calmly said, "I know."

Trudi's Journey Home

"I want to go home," said Trudi. "You're a good girl. You'll let me go home, won't you?"

Belinda was baffled. She had yet to be given the hospice literature which explained that dying people often speak in this way. Besides, Belinda refused to see that Trudi was a dying person. Two months before, she had written in her journal, "Trudi is absenting herself from life more and more." Somehow, Belinda had forgotten that insight now, as she rushed around fruitlessly, demanding a nausea remedy for Trudi and trying to procure food that she would eat.

The nausea medicine was belatedly prescribed—after the point when, unbeknownst to Belinda, Trudi had begun to spit out all her pills. In retrospect, Belinda felt ashamed of herself on account of all the food she had tried to cram into a dying woman, often causing her to cough and choke before giving up the struggle to swallow anything at all. "She's staying alive just for you," whispered Marty.

Then one day, Belinda arrived at the nursing home to find a woman with vacant eyes and slack mouth, already dwelling in some other realm. Belinda asked the head nurse to call hospice. Trudi pulled herself together when the hospice chaplain arrived: he spoke quietly to her about ordinary things, and she smiled. Yes, he should come back and sing to her; she would like that.

Later, Trudi and Belinda sat in front of Trudi's bedroom window in the late afternoon sun and watched the birds and squirrels. Belinda did not think, "Oh, this is the sunset of her life." She simply thought, "This is the end." Finally, Trudi turned to Belinda, her mouth in a rosebud grin and her eyes radiating self-knowledge. "Look at me," she silently conveyed: "I am beautiful, and I know what I am doing." It was her parting gift to Belinda.

18

Two weeks later, it was all over. The aides, the nurses, and the cleaning ladies hugged Belinda and told her they hoped they would still see her. "Oh, yes," she said. "Of course, I will come to see Leonard." What she did not say was that she could not yet give up the life-and-death drama of the nursing home.

Wasting Time: Love and Class

One day, not long before Trudi died, they were looking at her old photo album, the one she kept before she got married, the one that recorded the glamour of her young womanhood. Belinda marveled at the jodhpurs and the little pointy-toed boots Trudi used to wear to go horseback-riding. She must have paid for these luxuries out of the wages she earned as an unattached working girl, with no husband whose income needed to be supplemented or babies to help support. Looking at these pictures, Belinda thought that Trudi looked shy and pretty and hopeful, her whole life ahead of her.

Trudi put her finger on a tiny photo little bigger than a postage stamp. It was of a good-looking, seemingly self-confident young fellow, his wavy hair combed straight back and probably Bryl-creamed into place. "I can't remember his name," said Trudi, "but I was in love with him."

Belinda was silent. She had first heard about the one that got away many years before, when she was still a child, young enough to ask, innocently, "Why didn't you marry him, then?"

"He didn't ask me," Trudi had admitted. Case closed. Belinda did not want to force Trudi to say those words again, but her mind was full of questions: Had the young man merely been amusing himself by dating Trudi? Was she too poor or her family not respectable enough (with the father in the insane asylum, after all) to make a good match? Had Trudi been "in love" with either of her husbands? (That she came to love them, Belinda had no doubt.) When the young man in the picture disappeared out of Trudi's life, did she feel that he had wasted her time, preventing her from closing the deal with some more serious contender? By the time of her first marriage, to Leonard, she was already 27, a rather advanced age in the marriage market, especially for such a pretty girl.

Belinda remembered a severe lecture Trudi had administered, like a nasty dose of bitters, to her when she was a mere 18, having an innocent summer romance with a good-looking young truck driver who frequented the truck-stop diner where she worked. Trudi's point was not that the boy would take advantage of Belinda (one of Trudi's usual lines of attack), but just the reverse: that she was taking advantage of him. He was several years older, he might be looking for a wife, and he seemed serious about Belinda, but Belinda, for all her romantic pining, would never be a suitable mate for him. She was wasting his time, maybe even breaking his heart.

Belinda had been bewildered and angry. Of course she was not thinking about marriage; she was too young. She wasn't thinking about the future at all. She could scarcely get through the week. She did not foresee that Trudi would be proved right: that she would go back to school and forget all about her handsome truck driver, despite his pitiful letters.

Part II

Belinda Reflects

Missing Trudi

After the initial shock of learning that Trudi was not immortal after all and that Belinda lacked the godlike power to keep her alive, Belinda had felt more or less relieved that her mother was gone. The two women had loved each other, but had not liked or enjoyed each other all that much. Belinda liked to think that not all of her resentment of Trudi was produced by the appearance of a baby sister before Belinda was ready to accommodate a sibling, but she wasn't sure. Certainly, there had been other little points of contention, going all the way back to the fight over the glasses–Belinda's glasses and whether she got to wear them in a professional photograph being taken of the sisters.

Belinda was, perhaps, six; Delores 19 months younger. Trudi had sewn two fancy dresses out of some navy blue crinkly stuff, covered with tiny white cottony dots, for the occasion. Belinda, having worn spectacles from the age of three, felt that they were part of her face and, therefore, should be part of the picture. After all, she never went anywhere without them. But Trudi was adamantly opposed to having the picture she had in her mind, and which she had worked so hard to create with all that sewing, spoiled by the horn-rimmed look imposed even on small children at the time. It may have been the mother and daughter's first fight over what it meant to be a girl.

Belinda did not get to wear her glasses in the photo. She wore a scowl instead, and it is just possible that each woman had accumulated a list of petty grievances against the other that should have been forgotten long ago but somehow never was. Each had struggled to please the other, but met with little success, so that Belinda was more glad than sorry to give up the attempt.

And yet, every once in a while, Belinda would miss Trudi, both the sweet lady that other people saw and the quietly adventurous woman who had been mostly neutralized by age and disease. When spring had come after the hard winter, Belinda felt that Trudi should resurge like a perennial bloom, but knew that she could not, being contained in a jar buried under a pretty red tombstone in the Middleville cemetery. So, there would be no more driving to the lake or watching the birds or gazing admiringly at Ernest Sr's flowers, for Trudi. These were the things that Belinda missed.

The Gap Year

If she were a recent high school graduate, instead of a recent retiree, Belinda might be described as taking a "gap year"—a transition from one state to another. For the young person, the destination after the gap was usually higher education. But for Belinda, it was not at all clear what she should be doing or whether she needed to be doing anything in particular. In fact, she felt rather impatient with acquaintances who demanded to know, "What will you do with yourself *now*?," as if the only reason to live were to be perpetually busy.

Uneasily aware that casual observers might view her as an underachiever (What? No community service? No political canvassing?), Belinda nonetheless felt that her first year of retirement had been, in the words of Lady Bracknell, "crowded with incident." For one thing, there was the Trudi business and Belinda's disappointment that Trudi had turned out to be mortal like everybody else. Then there were her near-daily visits to Leonard, still over at the Lucky Stroke, which made her feel as if she were watching her own death. Belinda's own arthritic knee, which was becoming a project in itself, merely confirmed the idea that Belinda was already in a state of decline.

On a more positive note, there was the rapturous engagement of her son Ernest and his beloved Rafe. Two more besotted creatures she could not imagine. She was happy for them and duly announced the news to all and sundry, but in truth it took her a couple of days to *feel* that happiness. Her first uncontrollable reaction was to compare their bliss with her own slightly less blissful solitude and feel a little sorry for herself. She was not at all tempted, however, to go shopping for a mate. The young ones were taking the center stage where they belonged.

Part III

Men and Fathers

Imaginary Men

Just for fun, Belinda was in the habit of reading her daily horoscope. She was a Scorpio, "fiery and passionate," according to some long-ago-consulted source. She used to be those things, she thought, but how long could you keep that up?

Now, the relevant newspaper paragraph told her to make plans and follow them, not letting others dissuade her from what she wanted to do. What did she want to do, she wondered? Often the final sentence in the paragraph was something like "Romance is in the stars."

Romance might be in the stars, thought Belinda, but surely it was not here on earth with her. She could not think of a single man of her Middleville acquaintance who was both attractive and available, and the idea that she should seek romance online struck her as ludicrous and too much work. An old friend had once given her a refrigerator magnet that announced, "She liked imaginary men best of all." That was exactly right, for what were her long-term crushes on Sam Waterston and Placido Domingo if not confirmation of the fact that she had no interest in actual men at all?

Belinda realized that this was nothing to brag about, being one more symptom of life-long self-absorption, but she felt no urge to reform. Old ladies were supposed to talk to themselves—that is, to be their own best partners—and she supposed that was what she would become before long, an old lady, now that Trudi had died and taken away that buffer between Belinda and her own mortality. The fact that she had *always* talked to herself, had always done a running commentary on her own life, was, perhaps, beside the point.

Hey!

When Belinda visited the Lucky Stroke nursing home, she used to see two old men who roughly resembled one another sitting together in the dining room: bald but not decrepit, big-boned, tall, imposing— even in their wheelchairs. The more handsome of the two would always greet Trudi in a courtly manner, something she appreciated. Then he disappeared. Belinda wanted to think that he had been re-habbed out of there, but she knew better. Not long after that, Trudi disappeared too, and Belinda focused her attention on Leonard. (She was later to wonder whether an excess of that attention had the ef-fect of killing off her parents, but she knew she wasn't really that powerful.)

The other old man remained at his table in the dining room, and Belinda often greeted him as she did many of the old people, who had become familiar characters in her life. Then, one day, he began what Belinda would, melodramatically perhaps, describe as "stalking" her. While she was feeding Leonard, he would roll his wheelchair toward her table until some aide got him turned around. After lunch, he pursued her, telling her to count on him if anyone gave her trouble.

Belinda was not amused. She didn't care if she was considered ageist for being totally creeped out that some old guy in a wheelchair wanted to protect her. As far as she was concerned, he was just one more undesirable boy who had to be avoided at all costs. So she tried not to walk past his table, engage in eye contact, or even say "hello." After two days of this, he took action. "Hey!" he said, when she returned to the dining room to retrieve her coat after parking Leonard by the nurses' station. "Hey," she yelled back, before she fled through the nearest door.

Belinda rather admired his spirit. In a Hollywood movie, the Belinda character might reluctantly become his friend, showing that old people are real people too, deserving of love and respect. Of course, there would be nothing resembling sex in the portrayal. Still, Belinda had no desire to play such a role.

The next day, Belinda cautiously said "hello" when she walked past the old man's table. There was no glimmer of recognition in his stare.

Leonard in a Decline

Leonard was in a decline. Well of course he was. He had been officially diagnosed with Alzheimer's disease 16 years ago. Two years before that, Delores had whispered to Belinda, "I think Dad has Alzheimer's." Delores had expert medical knowledge, and Belinda generally believed what she said. Besides, the evidence was in front of them both: the repeated questions, the memory lapses that were more than just senior moments, the refusal to substitute for the vacationing organist at his church because public performance now frightened him. It didn't look good.

But 18 years ago, Leonard could still speak in complete sentences, compose music, sing arias (at least in the privacy of his own music room), and make love to his (second) wife, Grace. Even after Grace died from a terrible cancer, Leonard could still drive a car without getting lost and keep lunch dates with friends. Home care workers found him a witty and amusing companion, and he responded by proposing marriage to more than one of them.

It wasn't until 11 years ago that he started calling up Delores and Belinda to ask them where he was, where they were, and what had happened to his wife. Why was he all alone in a strange house? Belinda told her ex-husband that they had to go to Pennsylvania to kidnap Leonard and bring him back to Middleville, where the local assisted living unit had an opening. She even traded in her ancient sedan for a slightly used SUV in order to make the trip. By then, Leonard's memory was noticeably compromised, but he still managed to have a satisfying romance with a unit resident who imagined that he was her husband. When she died suddenly, he could not have told you why he was depressed, because he was missing someone he could not remember.

Then the physical deterioration set in, so that Leonard could no longer get out of bed by himself, rise from a chair, or even walk, let alone chase a pretty female aide around a dining room table, as he had previously tried to do. Belinda was told that she would have to find him an actual nursing home, a place not trying to make a profit by understaffing the facilities. Now Leonard had been at the Lucky Stroke nursing home for six years, and Belinda was a regular there, often feeding him his pureed lunch in order to keep up some sort of contact with a man who didn't know who she was.

Lately, though, he was forgetting or, perhaps, refusing to swallow. A year after Trudi had deliberately starved herself to death, Leonard was beginning a similar process through absent-mindedness. This made Belinda sad even though she knew he had outlived himself: good care had kept him alive too long. Still, she tried sometimes to emulate the patience of the young aide named Jenny, who was more successful than anyone else in persuading Leonard to "take a bite," to swallow, and to enjoy. Jenny was the sort of generous girl who paid to have neighborhood alley cats spayed just to reduce the amount of cat suffering in the world. She fed Leonard to give him one last bit of pleasure before he checked out altogether.

Belinda wasn't sure that Leonard could still experience pleasure. His face used to light up sometimes when she sang to him; now that seemed to be gone. He was winding down. It was time. She would not panic. She would search his files for the obituary he had written for himself years ago and revise it for an audience who had never heard of him before, because most of his friends had already died.

The Reinherz Men

Isaac

Belinda had told Leonard more than once, years before, when he was still an eager storyteller, that she knew more about his childhood than she knew about her own. This was a complaint. She had heard his stories, populated by larger-than-life characters, now mostly dead, more times than she could count.

"Why was this?' she asked him one evening. Why was he so fascinated by these people: his grandfathers, his parents, his uncles, even the family hangers-on?

"A fair question," he admitted, and theorized that, as a child with no siblings, who spent much time in the company of adults, he had been imprinted by them as only a child can be. They were powerful figures in his life, often in conflict with one another in ways he could not understand at the time. Now they were all drenched in nostalgia, no one more so than old Dr. Reinherz, his paternal grandfather, the family patriarch.

Isaac Reinherz had a thriving practice even though he couldn't give an injection worth a damn, especially as he got older and his hands became shaky. The thing was: he always seemed to know what was wrong with people and how to fix it. With his professional earnings and his rental properties, he could lose a pile of money in 1929 and still die rich in 1945, at least by middle-class standards. And then there was politics: Reinherz was chairman of the Brewer County Democratic Party apparatus for years, a position of some influence in the early decades of the century.

Altogether, Isaac Reinherz was a self-satisfied man who instructed his family members to address him as "Doctor" at all times, although his son Lyle, Leonard's father, was allowed to get away with "Pop," a minor act of rebellion. A visit to Isaac's parlor was an exercise in self-control and physical dexterity, for no child was allowed to let the bottoms of his presumably dirty shoes to touch the surface of the beautifully polished hard-wood floor, but must leap from carpet to carpet without disarranging the furnishings.

Young Leonard was unfazed by all these rules and often walked all the way from his parents' home in West Brewer to Isaac's office in the city, for the mere chance of spending ten minutes with the old man. Leonard knew he was the favorite grandchild, as the only bearer of the Reinherz name, his cousins being the off-spring of Isaac's daughter (and, therefore, automatically inferior).

When Isaac was ill with pleurisy in the Brewer Hospital, he summoned Lyle and Leonard to his bedside, not saying much, but gazing at them as if fixing them in his mind for all eternity. Leonard was clear: this was good-bye, even though Isaac's physicians expected him to recover. He died two days later, a few weeks after FDR, both losses crushingly great in Leonard's mind, so that he never stopped talking about either man for the rest of his life.

Lyle

Leonard's repeated paeans to his grandfather's glory made Belinda feel that the Reinherz family had been on a downhill slide ever since and that none of Isaac's descendants would ever be able to match him in achievement or obituary length in the local newspaper. Belinda understood that this was not Leonard's intent in telling his stories, which created a safe space for him to be, as his condition grew more fragile and present events slipped away from him.

Yet Leonard did seem to regard Isaac as representing a standard of excellence from which his own son Lyle, Leonard's father, fell short. Belinda knew that Lyle would himself have been regarded as a successful public man by most people—as president of the school board, member of the draft board, seller of big houses to rich clients in his prime, and, later, good-humored teacher in one of the last one-room country schoolhouses in Pennsylvania. It's true that the family received death threats on account of the draft board business, not a surprise, perhaps, given the number of immigrants in Brewer who still thought of Germany as the fatherland, even if they didn't much care for Hitler. Leonard, during this time, felt less frightened than neglected, as Lyle was never home, always, he said, at a meeting, but sometimes, Leonard suspected, busy conducting a flirtation (if not an affair) with Isaac's young wife, acquired many years after the death of Lyle's mother from cancer.

Belinda remembered her grandparents' beautiful twin beds with the pineapple motif and thought it likely that Lyle and her grand-mother Vicky had not had sex since Leonard's arrival in 1925. If Lyle had been a womanizer, Belinda was prepared to overlook it. He had been a good grandfather—smart, funny, and attentive. And if he had attempted to get even with his dictatorial father by romancing his stepmother, well, how Freudian of him! Surely, it was none of Be-linda's business. Perhaps Leonard just knew Lyle too well to fashion him into the kind of mythic hero he saw in his grandfather.

(No doubt, Vicky would have provided a different view of both men had anyone seen fit to ask her.)

Leonard's ambitions

Undaunted by what he took to be his grandfather's unmatchable achievements, young Leonard had aspirations of his own. He wanted to be a musician, and his parents never discouraged him from doing what others may have viewed as impractical. His mother Vicky was a musician too. She knew that her piano-playing abilities were not first-rate, but she had enjoyed providing the musical accompaniment to the silent movies of her youth and, later, to playing sheet music hits in Brewer's largest department store. She and Lyle were frequently the featured entertainment at neighborhood parties when she played and Lyle sang; people said he had a lovely voice.

But Leonard's talent was on a whole different scale. She could see that, so she bought a new upright and encouraged her son when he sought professional instruction in piano and voice. His facility with the former was remarkable, but, really, he was meant to become a singer. Already, in his teens, he was singing guest solos at all the major Protestant churches in Brewer and the tenor parts in locally performed oratorios. He would become a music teacher, of course, but she could see he had dreams of glory. As he grew up, she only wished she could help him more. She knew that he viewed his college voice teacher as inept. And then, after he graduated, he fell in love almost too fast with Trudi, the lovely girl from the German Lutheran church, where Leonard often sang solos. Soon there would be a marriage and babies, and Leonard would have to put all his energy into supporting his young family.

Still, Leonard did not give up: he had a plan. Belinda knew nothing about the plan when she came home from school one day and saw the sign sticking up like a bad weed in the front yard of their row house in Brewer. She was only 7, but she could read "For Sale," and she was upset. Their block was populated mostly by young families with kids; her boyfriend Harvey lived around one corner, and her girlfriend Ann lived around the other. She didn't want to move. And yet when they did move, a year and a half later, to the New Jersey suburb of Oakwood, it seemed like a great adventure (so persuasive was Leonard), and Belinda was sure that she would live in Oakwood for the rest of her life.

Belinda hardly listened to Leonard's compulsive speeches to Trudi about his new mentor in the city, a choral composer and teacher of voice. But even she noticed that this person was trying to forward Leonard's career, which was a hectic jumble of public-school teaching, church-choir directing, and private-lesson instruction. Looking back on this time, Belinda wondered how Leonard had had the energy to do all these things and drive to the city every week for study in vocal production and discussions which amounted to career counseling. The mentor secured an audition for Leonard at a major synagogue in the city, where he was offered the job of cantor on the spot, no need to learn Hebrew, they would spell the words phonetically for him, his was the voice they wanted. But Leonard and Trudi were trying to bring up the girls as Lutherans: how could he send them off to confirmation classes while he sang for people of a different faith?

In retrospect, Belinda thought this was a mistake—and not just because she had turned out to be an atheist while her sister verged on Buddhism (the confirmation classes having had an effect of limited duration)—but because it formed part of a pattern. Every time Leonard was offered what might have been his big break, he found what he regarded as equally compelling reasons not to take it. The fact is that he had come to the city too late. He was already in his 30's, with a family to support, and too much work. The window of opportunity for glory was already closing. He would become known, instead, for the achievements of his students and the choral societies he started wherever he went.

Wasn't this enough, wondered Belinda? Why did Leonard continue to tell those stories about Isaac, as if he were the only family member who had ever been successful? Maybe it was because, when Isaac was still alive, Leonard was still the golden prince who might accomplish anything.

Death of Lyle Reinherz

More than 35 years ago, Lyle had turned his face to the wall and stopped eating. He recognized no one and had no pleasure. He did not know where he was (the long-term care unit in the VA hospital nearest his home), and he did not wonder. He was done.

Yet his son Leonard and his wife Vicky could not let him go. Or, perhaps, a well-meaning physician persuaded them that a feeding tube would be just the thing. It was inserted, and Lyle's heart kept beating for several more years as the man sank into a coma, his body frozen in the fetal position. At Lyle's funeral in 1987, the casket was closed. He was 91.

"Don't worry. It wasn't Alzheimer's," Leonard tried to reassure the girls, and it's true that no such diagnosis had ever been made, Lyle's doctor preferring to suggest that the old fellow's dementia resulted from a vascular condition. The diagnosis was arrived at only in retrospect, fifteen years later when it became clear that Leonard himself was suffering from Alzheimer's, a family curse that put Belinda, Delores, and young Ernest all at risk.

Complaining that Alzheimer's sufferers were likely to be deprived of their human rights even before they lost their reason, Leonard did what he could to protect himself. He saw his attorney and made a Living Will. There would be no feeding tube for him when he reached Lyle's stage of incapacity. He would be allowed to die. It never occurred to him, or to anyone, that he would still be alive at 93, his daughters grieving for him—and for themselves.

Singing to Leonard

Belinda was standing at the beverage table pouring a glass of red Kool-Aid punch for Leonard when the old guy came up. He was a new resident, she thought, looking rather too physically fit to be nursing home material. Still, she ignored him at first, being skeptical about men in general, even old ones. This new guy, though, was not to be deterred by Belinda's rudeness. He put his walking stick next to hers and demanded her attention. "Are you the girl who sings to her father?" he asked. Belinda was politically incorrect enough to be gratified by being called a "girl." Of course, she understood that only in the nursing home would she be perceived as one.

"Yes, I am," she admitted. She had begun singing to Leonard more lately, more routinely, not primarily to stimulate his recognition of her any longer, but to wake him up enough to get him to eat a few bites. "Zip-A-Dee-Doo-Dah" was often good for a smile; "Oh What a Beautiful Morning" sometimes brought the smile close to tears. But on some days, he was too far gone to be reached, and maybe that was better. She didn't know whether she had the right to continue dragging Leonard back into the world of the living by making him feel.

Then, one evening, the singing ended. Leonard had been eating his supper with his eyes closed for years, but on this particular occasion he was alert. "How are you today, Dad?" queried Belinda. "Are you hungry?" He did not respond.

"Would you like some punch?" she persisted, bringing a spoonful of thickened red Kool-Aid to his mouth. He did not open. He calmly sat, lips together, eyes straight ahead, looking imperturbable. He refused all food, swallowed several spoonfuls of water, saying nothing, not appearing to recognize Belinda.

She did not sing to him. She did not try to will him back into the world by singing the old songs of her childhood that had often elicited a response from him. He looked so dignified that she did not wish to pretend that he was making some sort of mistake.

Yet maybe she was just fooling herself by imagining that he was making a deliberate choice. Nurse Heather said that he had gagged on the tiny bit of food she had gotten into him at lunch. Was this simply one more indignity of the disease and not an act of agency?

Belinda knew that it was time for Leonard to die, but she could not wish for it. She would miss him.

Leonard the Storyteller

Belinda listened to Leonard breathe and thought that she would remember him not only as a loving father and skilled musician, but as a great storyteller, a fabulist whose tales were filled with giants: larger-than-life characters like old Dr. Reinherz, Lyle, Vicky, and the Doctor's apparently irresistible wife Elinor. First seen through the eyes of Leonard the child, these figures never lost their epic glow.

Leonard, it is true, did not always approve of these characters: Vicky shammed illness to get attention; Lyle made passes at women who were not his wife; Doctor interrupted the church service every Sunday by entering his designated pew just before the sermon and leaving just after. But they were the heroes of his story nonetheless—not just protagonists but irreplaceable gods and goddesses in whose reflected glory Leonard's life took its meaning.

It's not that Leonard was not proud of his own accomplishments or those of his girls. But somehow these, valuable as they were, had not quite the glamour of those of his dramatic elders. Was it only nostalgia? Or was it that these elders had, in their prime, given him a sense of possibility? He could be great because Doctor smiled upon him; because he was inspired to be more faithful than Lyle; because he could become the musician that Vicky never had the chance to be.

Belinda thought that Leonard had told their stories better than any of them could have. What would these elders think of Leonard's life if they could see it whole? Vicky would be proud, Belinda was sure. She knew he had been a fine musician and a devoted son, husband, and father. Lyle might grouse that this was the end of the Reinherzes, no boys left to carry on the name. Doctor, Belinda imagined, would be philosophical, having enough laurels of his own to rest on: what did he need with those of his descendants? But Belinda wanted to explain to them—to all of Leonard's elders: no one remembered you as he did. No one could tell your story better or with more conviction that it was worth telling.

Maybe Belinda would become the storyteller now.

Part IV

Belinda Reflects

Staving Off Dementia

In an effort to stave off dementia, Belinda worked the daily crossword puzzle in the local newspaper, exercised at the gym, took Spanish lessons online (for a little while), and even (with many lapses) tried to eat more healthfully. She was doubtful that any of these measures would work, but she had become aware of a terrible tendency to blame the demented victim who had not subjected herself to such a regime.

Periodically, as part of its fundraising campaign, the public television station ran a series of probably bogus self-help documentaries targeted at baby boomers who had the disposable income to make donations to PBS. Belinda resented these shows not only for their obvious attempts to manipulate her age group, but also for the pseudoscience they engaged in. It was clear to her that the genial expert on "brain health" didn't really know what he was talking about when he described his regimen as a "choice" one could make not to become demented.

She wondered if she were really living if her days were taken up by staving off dementia. She had gotten better at the crossword puzzles and had learned any number of useless words that she would employ only in doing more crossword puzzles. She had lost a few pounds by exercising at the gym, but felt no more energetic than before. She had begun to eat green leafy vegetables with some regularity, and, no doubt, this couldn't actually *hurt*. Nonetheless, in some moods, she was appalled at what her life had become: a sort of holding action against despair.

Serena

Belinda was gratified to learn that, like herself, Serena Williams suffered from a sore left knee. It was not that Belinda wished anything ill for Serena; she was a hero worshipped even by Belinda who hardly ever noticed sports at all. It was only that if it was their disabilities alone—bad knees (now) and postpartum depression (long ago, for Belinda)—that linked them, Belinda would take that link as a token of sisterhood. Not being an athlete herself, Belinda did not have to worry that some ESPN commentator would nominate her for the "group of death," toward which poor Serena was prematurely being pushed. At 37, Serena was already confronting her mortality, at least as a tennis player.

Having reached the scandalous age of 69, Belinda thought, perhaps, that she would decide never to grow older. Like Jack Benny, stuck at 39, she would never admit to a birthday again, but just stay where she was. It was not until her early 70's that Trudi started having those undiagnosed little strokes. It was not until he turned 75 that Leonard started forgetting things and repeating himself in that most distressing manner. In some moods, Belinda thought she would like to avoid all that and skip the really bad stuff by freezing herself in time.

But in other moods, Belinda knew better. Eternal life, whether in this world or some other, really did not appeal to her. She was writing her thoughts down now because she knew she would not have them forever.

Belinda's Knee

Dr. O

Belinda was already on her feet when Dr. O walked through the door, 75 minutes late for her appointment. "I was meditating an escape," she said by way of explanation. She found his rather bewildered look satisfying. He was the orthopedic surgeon whose surgical skills she was trying *not* to use, and he was accustomed to a little more deference. On the other hand, he was still scolded by his mother from time to time, and Belinda looked distressingly like his mother.

Fortunately, Dr. O could assert himself more authoritatively before long. Belinda had prepared a typed list of questions about non-surgical treatments that could benefit her arthritic knee and he was, after all, an expert on this topic. Never mind, thought Belinda, that he could have made this information more available to begin with. And need he have made it so obvious that the dispensing of information was so much less interesting to him than the whipping out of a syringe and injecting her with something, as he had done on her first visit? Doubtless the insurance payments for injecting people were much greater than for giving them knowledge.

A project

Belinda was aware that her left knee had become a project, not the project she might have chosen, perhaps, but one with advantages of its own. It's true that she didn't like the pain or the disability caused by her arthritis, but on most days, the pain was not so great, and she found that her use of a cane inspired other people with age-related

45

maladies to tell her their stories. Then, there were her physical therapists, an upbeat, good-humored tribe who seemed like wise women in their ability to summon healing powers. Belinda felt that she had entered a different world in which the imperfections of the body became not so much a source of distress, but a down-to-earth way of coming to know oneself.

At first, she felt frustrated: how could she make plans to go anywhere or do anything? It's true that Dr. O's steroid shot had made her long-planned jaunt to the Big Apple do-able enough, especially with her son Ernest to help her by hailing cabs. But her usual pilgrimage to the DC fireworks on the 4th of July, involving much walking in sultry weather, had to be ruled out, as did any more physically ambitious adventure. This seemed like a bad thing, at first.

But, then, Belinda wondered: Did I really want to go to DC again when the temperature was likely to be 100 degrees? Do I necessarily want a more ambitious adventure? Maybe sometime. But she began to think that staying home, reading books, doing physical therapy, and socializing with the Lucky Stroke nursing home staff while she fed her demented dad his lunch were not such bad things to do. She actually began to feel happy.

Maybe Belinda's bad knee allowed her to do what she wanted, after all. She didn't have to go to Venice or Alaska or pretend that she loved travel. She didn't have to make a life plan for the next 5 years to prove that she wasn't just frittering her life away. It was hers to fritter. If able-bodiedness became a priority, there was always Dr. O and his knife. But she was still meditating her escape.

The Rooster Comb

Recovery

Once Belinda's bad knee became visible (because she wore a knee brace or carried a cane or sometimes used both; mere limping didn't do it), people began to give her advice: steroid injections, surgery, the rooster comb. The rooster comb?

Hyaluronic acid is no longer concocted out of rooster combs most of the time, which is a boon to people allergic to chickens, because it is now used widely to treat arthritic knees. "It works on only half the people," warned Dr. O, when Belinda asked him to inject the magic substance, hoping she would get lucky.

She had been told to expect a sensation of "pressure" on her knee afterwards; indeed, she felt, for a few hours, that her joint was encased in concrete. Then she would be in suspense for two weeks, during which time she had other, more urgent things to think about, for Leonard was clearly in a decline.

It just so happened that the day on which Leonard died was also the day on which Belinda found that the rooster comb had worked— that she was being granted a reprieve, a temporary extension of her stay in the land of the almost able-bodied. She was able to carry out the boxes of Leonard's few belongings from the nursing home to her car without difficulty, no cane required.

Her mortality had been unmistakably established, the decay produced by injury and age proved beyond a doubt by MRI and pain, but she would not, in the absence of freak accidents, be following Leonard into massive disability any time soon.

Walking to the P.O.

Months later, during the Covid pandemic, when every tiny episode seemed fraught with significance, Belinda walked to the post office one afternoon in March. She walked rather than drove because her knee threatened to become seriously stiff and lame again if she did not keep walking (the gym having been closed because of the virus). After she had mailed her bills and left the building, she saw an old friend approaching. They were delighted to see each other–more delighted than they would have been two months before, when they would have been happy enough. But, now, the new norms of isolation and social distance made every little exchange a vibrant oasis in the desert.

Dutifully, they began their conversation six feet apart, yo-yoing in to three feet, bouncing back to five. No one sneezed or sniffed; they scarcely even breathed.

"I went dancing last weekend," triumphed the friend.

"Good for you," Belinda grinned, remembering the folk-rock band she had gone to hear at that time.

"I had so much fun, but now all the dance clubs are closed," she lamented, striking a tango pose.

"It seems like we all knew that this past weekend would be the last normal one for a long time," said Belinda. Or maybe she just wanted to believe that she had not been taken totally by surprise at the necessary but life-constricting new customs that were now, nonetheless, producing exquisite moments of pleasure.

Peonies

In the painting, the peonies were life size in a white china vase sitting atop a wooden piece of furniture like a coffee table or cabinet. Dark red flowers predominated, but there were white ones too and a gorgeous pink right in the middle of the canvas. Belinda had never paid attention to the fact that there was a tiny dog in the picture as well, approaching the vase, its tail up and ready to wag, until artist friends, at one of her parties, mentioned it as a curiosity: Why make the dog so small and the flowers so large? What could the painter have been thinking?

The answer was simple, as far as Belinda was concerned. The artist hadn't portrayed a real dog at all, but a little ceramic dog of the sort painted by a bored housewife in a ceramics-painting class, where the molds were provided and the goal was to apply the paint as precisely and prettily as possible. Belinda's grandmother Vicky excelled at such work, and her house, as well as Leonard and Trudi's, was littered with the resulting objects. As a girl, Belinda rather liked these figurines, not yet understanding that the more cultivated consumer might consider them kitsch.

If Lyle's cousin Elda, the painter of the peony picture, saw fit to include the little dog, perhaps it was because the peonies might well have had to share space with him on the middle-class coffee table of the day, sometime in the middle of the 20th century. Belinda didn't know whether Lyle had commissioned this picture from his cousin, a regional artist of some repute, or simply purchased it from her after the fact. Or maybe it was a present because she knew he liked to grow peonies.

Belinda thought the flowers in the painting, representing various stages of perfect ripeness and incipient decay, exuded a passionate vitality that only living things are supposed to do. (And maybe the inclusion of the little dog did enhance this effect.) But she had seen this painting on one wall or another her entire life.

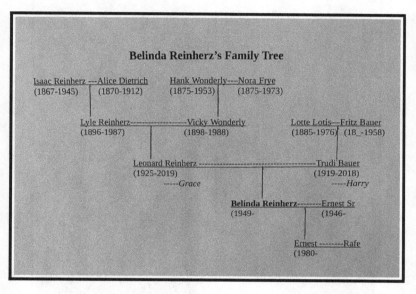

Belinda Reinherz's Family Tree

Isaac Reinherz ---Alice Dietrich
(1867-1945) | (1870-1912)

Hank Wonderly---Nora Frye
(1875-1953) | (1875-1973)

Lyle Reinherz-------------------Vicky Wonderly
(1896-1987) | (1898-1988)

Lotte Lotis---Fritz Bauer
(1885-1976) (18_-1958)

Leonard Reinherz ---------------------------------------Trudi Bauer
(1925-2019) (1919-2018)
-----Grace -----Harry

Belinda Reinherz--------Ernest Sr
(1949- (1946-

Ernest --------Rafe
(1980-

"Reinherz" Family Tree

"Lotte" and "Fritz"

"Isaac"

"Leonard"

"Lotte"

"Trudi"

"Trudi" and "Leonard" Wedding

"Hank" and "Nora" holding "Belinda"

Part V

Orphans

Surprised by Death

"Fire or water?" asked Dorothy. Water cremations were believed to be more environmentally friendly, and Dorothy was proud of her new technology. You submerged the body in a bath of hot water and lye for a number of hours, speeding up decomposition, and were left only with bone. The bone was then dried, air-dried in Dorothy's establishment, and pulverized into beautiful cream-colored sand. As long as you didn't think too hard about your loved one being cooked as if in a stew, there was a certain appeal to the whole process. Belinda could imagine Dorothy reverently laying out the bones, reducing them to the lovely powder that would go into an urn. Wouldn't this be better than the fiery inferno or the embalming fluid that preserved what ought not to be?

"Water," said Delores, and Belinda agreed. They had come to Dorothy's sanctum in the first place so that Delores, fresh off the plane from Seattle, could see Leonard one last time before the cremation. Belinda had seen him already the preceding day at the nursing home and did not know that she needed to see him again.

The thing is that no one looks one's best when surprised by death. One's eyes are likely to be open, staring sightlessly. The mouth is poised for one last breath. The will of the body to remain alive overrides the individual's desire for dignity. One has no time to compose oneself. This, then, becomes the undertaker's job: to restore the dignity of the departed loved one so that the living may say good-bye.

When Delores saw Leonard, she was appalled, at first, by his marble composure, the fun-loving dad clearly gone. But Belinda murmured, "Oh, he looks so good," for he looked stately, even noble, she thought, with his broad forehead, straight nose, and generous mouth, frozen into statuesque calm. She had to restrain herself from asking

60

Delores to take his picture. Later such an artifact would feel macabre, she was sure. It was better to keep this last image only in her mind.

Late Summer

Middleville had reached that icky part of the summer when large clumps of cat hair were visible on the carpet 36 hours after the last vacuuming and small bugs died in Belinda's morning brew. Cicadas sang desperately every evening, pleading for sex before their time was up.

Back when she was a professor at Middleville State, Belinda would take these things as tokens of impending work ahead: syllabi to be made, new university policies to be learned, computer innovations to be ignored. For years, she had loved going back to school in the fall, even if she could not quite convince herself that August was the fall.

Now she was glad that she could listen to the cicadas' song without feeling that her time was running out. Instead, it stretched ahead of her as if she were on a plain and she would live until she reached the ever-receding horizon, like Tennyson's Ulysses.

Ulysses imagined that he would have one more great adventure, win another war, maybe, or at least stage a decent battle. Or perhaps the goal was just to get out of the house because Penelope was not as much fun to live with as to think about when he was on the road. Anyway, Ulysses wanted his old cronies to hang out with him, even if Homer tells us they had all been lost in one way or another. Maybe they existed only in the old man's mind, rambling old codger that he was. Did he suffer from dementia too?

Perhaps Belinda would not follow him after all.

Living with the Dead

Belinda sat on her bed and drank mocha. She read the *Times*. She wrote in her journal, happy that she did not have to leap up, throw on some clothes, and drive down to the Lucky Stroke nursing home 15 miles away.

At the same time, she was—not exactly sad not to go there but—maybe a little lost, unmoored in the universe. She thought about what Delores had said on the phone when she first heard of Leonard's passing: "We're orphans." It wasn't just a truism, but a diagnosis. "Rather elderly orphans," Belinda had replied ruefully. "Yes," agreed Delores; "most people go through this when they are much younger," reminding her sister that there was something to go through. Belinda remembered how Leonard had wept at his mother's funeral even though he was already in his 60's and Vicky had reached 90.

A friend in the neighborhood put it more bluntly, "Things will look different to you when you are next in line to die." His own parents had died many years before and he had been predicting his own death ever since, but Belinda could not discount his words.

Her mind was filled with dates relevant only to dead people—and herself: Vicky's birthday (coming up), Leonard's birthday (two days after that), Trudi and Leonard's anniversary (not celebrated since their divorce in 1982). Psychologists called it proactive inhibition when the data cluttering your mind prevented you from learning new information of a comparable sort. Whose birthday did she fail to remember because Trudi's would never be dislodged from her brain? Perhaps this was too literal-minded an interpretation of the phenomenon. Maybe it was more to the point to recognize that older people became older partly because they could not help living with the dead.

Creating Safety

Leonard had done a good job of making the girls feel safe. When the family went to see *On the Beach*, a Cold War film in which all the characters were dying of radiation sickness following a nuclear war, Leonard told them: "Don't worry. It will never happen. It's too far-fetched." Belinda, who had never considered duck-and-cover exercises at school as any more meaningful than fire drills, was easily reassured. If Delores disagreed, she kept her own counsel.

Later, Belinda recognized that her childhood had always seemed safe because her parents had inspired this feeling. Leonard, in particular, had been the voice of optimism, Trudi having had some youthful experiences that would long haunt her. Yet, even as a child, Belinda understood that Leonard had anxieties of his own—worries about everyday things, the sort of minutiae that would eventually come to plague Belinda as well (signs of an anxiety disorder, perhaps?). In any case, Belinda knew about Leonard's worries because she had eavesdropped while he confided in Trudi, who mostly listened tolerantly, but occasionally grew impatient with the confessions of a neurotic who had no real problems. Still, even if Belinda knew that Leonard's optimism was a front (too many readings of *The Power of Positive Thinking*, she thought), she had counted on it—even after the Alzheimer's kicked in.

When she and her ex, Ernest Sr, drove to Pennsylvania to kidnap Leonard and bring him back to an assisted living unit for Alzheimer's patients in Middleville, the idea was to make *him* safe. He had been living by himself, a widower who had never learned to cook, was no longer allowed to drive, and was inadequately served by well-meaning aides who came to his house a few hours a week. Delores and Belinda worried about him all the time. But when Leonard was established in his Sunny View room, the person who benefited the most from this arrangement was not Leonard at all, but Belinda.

She would not have admitted this at the time, and she often complained to Leonard that she could not stand one more Dr. Reinherz story or another tale about how much fun he had had in college. But the fact remained that it was Leonard who was the person happiest to see her on any given day, the person who made her feel safe again in the universe. For Belinda had been having a hard time: her personal life in shambles, her age a source of discontent, her work a mixed bag of pleasure and discord. Even she recognized that she was undoubtedly mildly depressed. After trying one kind of psychotropic drug, which made her feel worse, she decided not to experiment with other chemical remedies, but to wait for time and events to make her feel better. In retrospect, she could see that it was Leonard who had made her feel better. She had often resented his need of her, not fully understanding that he anchored her to the earth in a way that made her secure. She remained, for him, the young person for whom anything seemed possible—the person, maybe, he used to be.

Now, in the wake of Leonard's death, she would, at last, have to become a grown-up who made her own safety—and found her own fate.

Talking to the Dead

People kept asking her, "what do you do with yourself all day?" Not wishing to appear either religious or delusional, Belinda did not answer, "I talk to the dead." She did not imagine that Trudi or Leonard was looking down upon her from heaven (or any other place). Nor was she subject to ghostly hallucinations of the Topper variety. She knew that the dead existed only in the minds of those who remembered them, which seemed reason enough to think about them now, when she could still remember them.

She would not resurrect them if she could, certainly not into the suffering bodies they had had at the end. The body was not made for immortality, even if the brain, at times, persuaded its owner that he yearned for it. The songs and stories Leonard had chosen for his funeral were full of promises of eternal life. Belinda remembered his reasoning on the subject, which he had explained to her when she was just a girl: "Why would a loving God give us life if only to let us die in the end? There must be more." But what if you took the "loving God" out of the picture? Then what?

Consciousness brought suffering, Buddhists and Romantic poets agreed. Conversely, suffering made one too self-aware. The happy person forgot herself, ignored her pain as much as she could. Belinda was grateful that she could still forget herself at times, that her pains did not outweigh her pleasures, which still seemed substantial. But witnessing the declines of Trudi and Leonard had made her fearful that she would suffer as long and as hard as they had—and with much less grace.

The Wedding Photo

They are just two young kids, frozen in time, posing for their wedding photo, taken by the best professional photographer in Brewer, the husband of one of Lyle's many cousins. Still only 21, Leonard appears as a skinny youth, thinner than Belinda ever saw him in life, improbably dressed up in tails. He has a full head of hair, which he would gradually lose, and the full lips he would keep until death. Trudi, at 27, looks no older, as if her features were still taking shape, to form her greatest beauty in middle age. The train of her elegant gown is arranged in folds in front of her.

The bride in her white dress is a beacon of light in the classic black-and-white photo, the two tentatively happy people (their smiles cautious) surrounded by darkness in the old German Lutheran church to which Trudi belonged (and where Belinda herself would, one day, be married). A white altar, shining with ornate carvings, a large bouquet of flowers on top, stands behind them, the steps on which they stand invisible.

Seventy-one years later, Belinda would say to Trudi, "It's June 1st. Do you remember what happened on that day?"

"I got married," said Trudi without hesitation. "It's my anniversary." They were in the Lucky Stroke dining room, where Leonard, her ex-husband since 1982, sat with his eyes closed, waiting for someone to bring him his food.

But in 1947, Trudi and Leonard Reinherz were still immortal, beautiful young people who would never grow old, despite having just got married and, therefore, achieving that then-obligatory gateway into full adulthood. Leonard had to get serious about earning money, now that he had a wife to support. Trudi never gave up her earning power; nonetheless, she put away her jodhpurs and settled

67

into being a wife, warning Leonard that there must be no baby for the first year. (Leonard's big wild collie was bad enough.)

Belinda remembered that they were still passionate about each other in her early childhood. One day, she caught them in a romantic clutch and had to squirm her way between them so as to be included. A few years later, Trudi would be ironing late in the evening and Leonard would call plaintively from their room, "Come to bed, Trudi! Come to bed!" Trudi would ignore him and go on ironing while Belinda wondered innocently what he wanted.

Now that Trudi and Leonard were both gone and Belinda seemed bent on turning them into works of art, she thought she would get the wedding photo framed and let the two young people it portrayed, strangers in a way, speak to her as they would.

Christmas Eve with the Reinherzes

Pearls

It was Christmas Eve, some year in the 1960's, and the Reinherzes were opening presents, the girls, almost in their teens, having got too old to believe in Santa Claus. Besides, Leonard would have to play the organ at the Lutheran Church in the morning, so it was better to have family time now.

He watched in anticipation as Trudi opened her gift from him, a beautiful rope of pearls. "Oh, they're lovely," she said, the yearning in her voice palpable. He felt thankful and relieved, knowing the pearls were a risk. But then a different mood set in, and Trudi said, "We can't afford them. You'll have to take them back."

"It's only money," muttered Leonard.

Why couldn't she ever accept just one of his gifts with a good grace?

Money

Belinda looked at her sister Delores, who shook her head.

"Why does she always have to be so mean to him?" said Belinda when the girls reached their room.

Delores was Trudi's favorite; Belinda was Leonard's. It gave them different perspectives. "You know she works to support the family too," said Delores. "It's not just him. So it's like she's paying for her own present when she could be spending that money on something she needs more."

Belinda nodded. "He always says Trudi works just because she'd be bored if she didn't. But I know that isn't right; we need the money." Belinda was notoriously bad with money herself, squandering her allowance on the day it was dispersed, then begging for handouts if something came up later in the week. Her sister, by contrast, tended her funds faithfully, going to work in the local supermarket as soon as she was old enough, thereby managing to buy an aging clunker of a car right after she got her license at the age of 17.

Belinda would not drive until she was 33 and had taken a temporary job in a tiny village in Wisconsin, where there were fewer people on the road to be run over and, therefore, less chance of accidentally committing vehicular homicide. Even worse, she did not think seriously about money until still later, when her son Ernest was in grade school, she had left Ernest Sr, and she began to understand what it meant to be the family breadwinner. She was aided in this recognition when she had the following dream: she and Ernest were in a car together which seemed to be going all over the place with no definite destination because no one was actually driving it. She woke up in a sweat—and took the dream as a sign that she needed to become more responsible.

Class

Trudi was mortified. She was angry with Leonard for having turned her into a shrew one more time. She was also angry with him for trying to behave like the rich guy he thought he should be, buying his wife expensive presents when, in fact, any large outlay would have to be subsidized by Trudi herself in one way or another. She knew Leonard and the girls were sick of hearing the story about how she would get one orange for the holiday when she was a girl: the family was that poor. But she hadn't minded. After all, the family had moved from a one-room hut with a dirt floor in East Prussia to a roomy row house in Brewer.

As a child, Trudi had never felt poor in Brewer. But her family was ambitious for her. Lotte had tried to warn her against marrying Leonard: he was too young, six years younger than Trudi, not yet a good provider, living still with his parents. Did Trudi want to begin her married life in her in-laws' attic? Yes, he sang nicely, but what did he get paid for that?

Trudi couldn't even maintain that she was passionately in love with Leonard. The fact was that his was the only eligible offer she had received, and she was already 27. He was a nice boy, earnest and sweet. She thought she could make a life with him; anyway, she would have to try.

No doubt, she had been only vaguely aware of how odd the Reinherzes, with their established name in the community, would have found it (had they known) that Trudi's poor immigrant family had assessed Leonard's earning power and found it wanting—indeed, had found him wanting as a mate for their girl. Yet Leonard sensed that his new mother-in-law was not his fan.

The fact that he and Lotte quietly disliked one another for the rest of Lotte's life was problematic enough: Trudi could see that Belinda had adopted her father's attitude of faint social snobbery toward the old woman. But the money part was worse—and maybe even more complicated, thought Trudi—than her mother had anticipated. Leonard, in fact, worked very hard to be a good provider, supplementing his modest public-school teacher's pay with church work and private lessons. Nonetheless, he seemed to feel that it was beneath his dignity to worry very much about money. He acted, sometimes, as if he were descended from some sort of aristocrat, his grandfather old Dr. Reinherz, from whom he had inherited nothing, except a sense of entitlement.

Vicky and Her Twins

Vicky would never get over the loss of her twins. One was still-born and she never even saw it. The other was a beautiful little girl who lived only a few hours; in 1923 she was just too tiny and delicate to live longer. She would be buried as Infant Daughter Reinherz in the family plot.

Vicky felt that her body and soul had been torn apart in a way no man could understand, certainly not Lyle. It was true that Lyle's stoic response to his own and other people's suffering might be more of a pose he learned as a medic during the war, but she could see he was not about to drop it now. He pitied her and retreated from her sorrow, not wishing to be reminded of his own grief at the death of their first babies.

Prostrate from blood loss and mourning, Vicky went home to her parents, Hank and Nora Wonderly, to be nursed back to health. Lyle came by nearly every evening and smoked with Hank, while Nora fed Vicky until she was strong in body if not in mind.

Nora was a country woman who understood that tragedy was part of life, you couldn't avoid it, but you could snatch what pleasure offered itself. She knew she'd never live down that little affair she'd had a few years back with Hank's best friend Ben. No harm had been done, she thought: she and Hank and Ben were still best friends (and much later Belinda would see their three tombstones lined up together at the cemetery). But Nora's younger daughter Mona had learned of the infidelity and told her mother she was not respectable. Of course, that had never been Vicky's line, but Nora could see that Vicky was trying to be a lady to suit the rich doctor's son she had married. All Nora could do was to heal the bruised darling as best she could so that Vicky and Lyle could try again.

72

A couple of years later, when Leonard was born, bawling and healthy, everyone heaved a sigh of relief. Nonetheless, the forceps delivery left Vicky in need of "repair," and she was instructed not to get pregnant again. Pining for siblings, Leonard was told the story of the twins, and took refuge in his collie instead.

Lyle and Vicky remained fond of each other, Belinda was sure, but sex between them may have become just too problematic, the cause of dead babies and a damaged womb. Yet they appeared socially as a handsome couple, Vicky and Lyle, that pinched look that showed up on their faces in photographs taking decades to arrive.

Lyle the War Medic

The car ahead of them skidded off the wet road and crashed into a ditch. Lyle assessed the situation quickly: he could devote his energy to helping the crash victim now emerging shakily from her car, blood spurting from her forehead, or waste time preventing Vicky from going into a dead faint. "Leonard," he ordered, "take your mother to that farmhouse just ahead and tell the people there to call an ambulance. I'm going to help this lady."

Lyle made the woman sit down, gave her his clean handkerchief, and told her to press it against her wound. Then he retrieved the first aid kit he always had in his car and bound up her gash with the calm expertise he had acquired as a war medic fifteen years before. "You're going to need stitches," he told her.

"I was going too fast," she admitted. "I didn't realize the road was still so slick from the rain." Lyle said nothing, but made a mental note not to let Vicky take up driving.

"Oh, God, there's my husband—he'll be mad," she said as a sedan pulled up with a worried-looking man at the wheel and Leonard and Vicky sitting next to him. The woman had crashed close to home.

"Your wife needs stitches, the sooner the better," said Lyle. "Take her to the Brewer Hospital and let them look her over." Lyle adopted the authoritative tone that made most people do what he said.

"Pop," said Leonard when they were safe back at home in West Brewer, "why didn't you become a doctor like my grandfather? Accidents and blood don't bother you."

"Oh, I fixed up enough bloody people in the war to last me a lifetime. When I got back from France, all I wanted to do was marry your mother and get a job, not spend years in medical school." Lyle returned to reading the newspaper, an indication that the conversation was closed. He never discussed his war experiences with anyone, let alone a sensitive boy like Leonard or a tender-hearted woman like Vicky.

A few years back, his war trauma had caught up with him, and he walked about with visions of horror frequently before his eyes, until old Doctor Reinherz, intuiting what was wrong, prescribed a rest cure at Ocean Grove, New Jersey, where Lyle spent three of the most boring weeks of his entire life. He understood that unless he could suppress his demons and model normality, he would never be allowed to return to Vicky and Leonard, so he did his best to appear what he was supposed to be. He came back to his family apparently cured, one more victory for the old doctor, Leonard would tell his daughter, much later. For Lyle's self-possession would remain secure until many years later when dementia set in and he would ask Belinda, "Have you seen my parents? I can't find them. I don't know where my parents are."

Hank Wonderly

Lyle claimed that he could never forgive Nora for breaking Hank's heart, or so he said in his later years, seeming to forget the role he had himself played in the heartbreak department. Belinda could not, in fact, remember Hank, he having died when she was only three, but pictures of him and Leonard's stories about his maternal grandfather suggested a rather jolly figure, possibly Nora's equal in adventurous behavior.

Belinda had little doubt that Hank had been a stagecoach driver in his youth or that he had become a prize-winning insurance salesman during his later, more respectable years (although Leonard did tend to glorify the elders he was fond of). What was not so clear to her was whether he really had been a small-time bootlegger during Prohibition who, when apprehended by the authorities, suffered minimal punishment because of his immense popularity in the community.

Vicky was embarrassed, of course, said Leonard, and Belinda understood that Vicky and her sister Mona had tried to distance themselves just a bit from their not-entirely-well-behaved working-class parents and the *menage a trois* they produced by running a boarding house in a sturdy, but cramped West Brewer dwelling. (Nora's lover Ben was the boarder who rarely left home.)

Isaac Reinherz may have been the admirable grandfather in Leonard's eyes, Belinda thought, the one who had achieved success (and merited a page-one obituary in the local paper), but Hank was the one who had time for the boy and did not send him home after ten minutes. Later, Leonard had mourned the way Hank had faded away and lost his vigor long before his death on January 1, 1953, celebrating the new year with a major cardiovascular event.

Vicky, Nora, and Lyle

Belinda had been just a kid but old enough to understand the phrase "venereal disease" when Lyle walked around the house muttering it. Vicky's mother Nora had a urinary tract infection, a common affliction among old ladies, but Lyle preferred to think of her as a hussy who brought all maladies of her nether parts upon herself even if she was eighty-something. Later, Belinda would think that his real objection to Nora was that she wouldn't follow the rules about how women were supposed to behave. She said what she wanted and did what she wanted, the opposite of Vicky, who had allowed Lyle to tyrannize over her for fifty years or more.

It was true that, by the time Nora went to live with Vicky and Lyle, she had mellowed considerably, having become a handsome old woman with snow-white hair and twinkling blue eyes, who had no controversial opinions about anything and watched *Lassie* on TV every Sunday night. Still, her very presence in his house was a kind of blight, demanding Vicky's time and attention, and siphoning off her love.

Vicky herself felt conflicted. Her husband and her mother both wanted all her care for themselves, and each seemed stronger than she was. She resisted sending Nora to the county old folks home, but gave in when she saw that the place had its own little society in which her mother might thrive. Besides, Lyle gave her no peace, arguing that her care of Nora was running her ragged, never understanding that it was his incessant harping on this theme that came close to finishing her.

Nora, in fact, did well in the nursing home, playing cards, flirting with the men, and making conversation until her hearing gave out entirely. She was 98 when she lapsed into unconsciousness, a prelude to her final sleep.

Vicky moped around the house, jumping every time the phone rang. She had passed her driver's test many years before, but Lyle had never subsequently allowed her to drive, so there was no way she could readily get to her mother's bedside. She knew better than to pester Lyle, who would be sure to say, "We just went two days ago. She wouldn't notice you anyway. Just take it easy. Don't upset yourself."

Vicky tried not to weep. Her mother was dying, and she could see that some great change was coming over Lyle. The last time they drove to the hospital, he had almost gotten lost, and she had had to remind him of the way. She was 75 years old, and soon there would be no one left who knew what she knew or could remember what she remembered.

Alice D

The woman in the photograph is not beautiful; the nose, perhaps, is slightly too large. But her generous mouth and shining dark eyes create an impression of vitality that offsets the school-marmish look of her Victorian collar and hairstyle. Alice Dietrich Reinherz died in 1912, at the age of 42, from cancer Belinda had heard, but the fact was that no one now living could remember her.

Years ago, Lyle would speak of her, his mother (Belinda's great-grandmother), from time to time, with reverence and gratitude. He had been very ill as a boy with typhus (or was it typhoid?), and his convalescence had taken a long time. He credited Alice's devoted nursing with saving his life. He was only 16 when she died.

She had lost two children in between the birth of Lyle's older sister Leda in 1891 and Lyle himself in 1896. They had been in the toddler stage of development, maybe just too young to fight off whatever fever afflicted them. Did that heartbreak make her even more careful of Lyle? How could it not? But little children died all the time, still, in the 1890's, like Lotte's siblings who succumbed to smallpox.

Belinda wanted to thank Alice for saving Lyle, if that is what she did, and for making him feel loved because there was no doubt about that. She also wanted to thank Alice for passing on her imperfect good looks, which had stamped themselves upon all of her descendants. Leda had been almost a carbon copy of her mother, while Lyle combined the somewhat dour physiognomy of his father with his mother's more outgoing mien. Lyle had been handsome, as Belinda's son Ernest was now.

It was impossible to know what Dr. Reinherz had thought of his first wife. Neither of the two obituaries of the doctor, pasted into Leonard's scrapbook, even mentions that Alice had ever existed. It is true that the doctor had waited a long time to re-marry, but was that out of love for Alice or dislike of the institution that had united them? There was no way to know.

Leda named her only daughter Alice, and Belinda seemed to remember some talk that Vicky's daughter would have been named Alice, too, had she lived. Now Alice's influence, if it still existed at all, was subterranean, Belinda's curiosity piqued only by an old photo and a half-remembered story.

Moments of Delight

When old Dr. Reinherz had been in the hospital with pleurisy, it was expected by others that he would recover. Then one evening he apparently fell out of bed and hit his head, resulting in a nasty contusion that even the art of the undertaker could not conceal. He died the same night.

Lyle did not request an investigation. The hospital was the one in which Doctor had himself practiced, and Lyle did not wish to cause trouble. His father was old and tired and ready to make an end; indeed, he had summoned Lyle and Leonard to his bedside to offer a tacit farewell a few days before.

Studying Doctor's obituary photo long after these events had occurred, Belinda was struck by how closely it resembled a death mask, the weight of the world seeming to press upon the old man's shoulders, the faithful physician who, in the quaint language of the *Brewer Times*, "did not enjoy a vacation in 35 years." (Did he take vacations but not enjoy them, wondered Belinda?)

Perhaps, then, it was not a totally outlandish conclusion for Leonard to reach, in the early years of his Alzheimer's struggle, that his grandfather had committed suicide. Of course, Belinda pointed out how unlikely that would have been. Throwing oneself out of bed was hardly a reliable method. Even had Doctor managed to hit himself on the head with a blunt object, as Leonard suggested, the result would have been iffy. But Leonard wanted to believe that the old man had remained in charge of his own destiny to the end. More to the point, he wanted to believe that he could too.

The thing is that no one wanted Leonard to kill himself when he still had the capacity to do so. Belinda and Delores were horrified at the idea that the Doctor story seemed to portend. Even Leonard himself, daunted by the course his disease was likely to take and grief-stricken at the loss of his beloved wife Grace (whose death from cancer came shockingly fast), remained his essential self: an optimist who could flirt with suicide but never actually do it.

If some Dickensian ghost (or hallucination) had come to him at the age of 78 (the age at which his grandfather had died) and shown him the sixteen years still ahead of him—the years in which he would say plaintively "My brain doesn't work," followed by the years in which his legs didn't work, and then the years in which even speaking became a challenge—would Leonard, then, have taken the final drastic step? Or would he have said to himself, as undoubtedly he did say, "But I still feel moments of delight?"

Part VI

Weddings and Funerals

Funerals

Harry Heiter had lived in Cedarton his entire life, and he was so gregarious that he could not go into the supermarket for one item—strawberries, say—without coming across an old friend and talking to him for 45 minutes. Thus, his funeral, well planned out and paid for in advance, was bound to be a success. When he died suddenly of a pneumonia case made deadly by the lung cancer Harry had preferred not to know about (a brilliant move on his part, thought Belinda), there were plenty of Cedartonians and assorted relatives to mourn his loss even though he was nearly 89 years old. The funeral parlor was sociably crowded.

Trudi was at her best, self-possessed and charming, telling the guests Harry would be saving her a place in heaven. Worried about the future—Trudi's future without Harry—Belinda marveled that Trudi could be so calm. Belinda herself was in a state of shock, having seen Harry only ten days before his death when he seemed quite jolly, walking about with his oxygen tank trailing behind him, apparently stable. Now his body, looking rather diminutive without his endless stream of talk to enlarge him, was all but smothered by an enormous pile of coffin bedding, as if to keep him warm.

Certainly, he was present in a way. A funeral starring the creepily dead body did have the advantage of convincing the attendee that the departed one really had died and was not simply vacationing in Daytona Beach. An urn filled with cremains was not nearly so persuasive. Just about anything could be in there, and whatever was in there bore little resemblance to the walking-around person that you knew. When, several years later, Belinda placed Trudi's urn into the ground, she felt that the essence of Trudi really was gone, that this jar of ashes had no magic power.

Leonard's service was still to come, water cremation having already reduced him to sand (pulverized bone) rather than ash, but this time Belinda would put her faith in art rather than the remnants of the body. Leonard's hymns would allow her to celebrate him for the moments that she participated in singing them, and she would weep while Ernest read Tennyson's "Crossing the Bar" (Leonard's favorite death poem because it had been his grandfather's).

The Wedding

A study in black and white, Ernest wore a black dinner jacket into which were woven images of small white ducks. His shirt was white and starchy-looking, topped by a ruffled black bow tie. His pants were black, matched by black cloth loafers. Rafe had the same shoes, tie, and shirt, but wore a white jacket edged in red and blue. The two looked at each other adoringly. Then Emilie began to speak.

She was going to make them husband and husband, having obtained the requisite certificate to do so online at their urging. They knew she would put on a good show, and she did. She had interviewed both Ernest and Rafe in depth about the history of their relationship, and she told the story of how the lovers had met on Halloween nearly two years before in a gay bar having a jock-strap contest. Rafe was dressed up as the Queen of Spades, but Ernest had actually donned a jock-strap for the occasion.

"What?" thought Belinda. "I've never heard this part of the story before." Presumably, Ernest had worn something in addition to a jock strap on a cool October evening. Anyway, everyone was laughing. Why have a big queer wedding if you could not tell the truth—or, at least, part of it?

Emilie accomplished the legal part of the ceremony quickly and finished up with a song of her own composition. She sang well and accompanied herself on the ukulele, encouraging audience participation. Although Emilie would admit to being an adherent of wicca, no religion of any kind was invoked at the wedding. There were no prayers, no marching down the aisle (there was no aisle), and no worries about who would obey whom. There were just two still-youngish men rapturously in love and a crowd of friends cheering them on, in a candle-lit restaurant where everyone soon sat down to share a meal.

Later, Belinda would remember her own nuptials in the same German Lutheran church where Trudi and Leonard had been married, Ernest Sr having nixed the idea of a courthouse procedure. Belinda had hated pretending to be a Lutheran, although she had been raised as one, and she despised being forced to attend the religious instruction sessions that no one took seriously, certainly not the minister, who was notorious for cheating on his spouse. When Belinda objected to promising wifely obedience, Rev. Starch just laughed— before telling her that, of course, the Lutheran ceremony no longer included this outmoded phrase, it being 1974.

Still, she did have to wear the white dress (in preparation for which she starved herself the one and only time in her life), march down the aisle on her father's arm, and be "given away" by her parents. She remembered thinking, even in the midst of the proceedings, "What the hell am I doing?" This unbidden reaction was not to the choice of her mate, but to the lack of freedom the married state represented in her mind, especially to women. She had gotten married because she was supposed to, and she had loved Ernest Sr possibly as much as she could love a husband. Maybe she was just too self-absorbed to love a mate as unambivalently as Rafe and Ernest appeared to love each other. But maybe, also, heterosexual marriage really was the problematic institution she believed it to be, often perpetuating gender roles that had grown too small.

Marriages

Leonard at the Door

Leonard stood knocking at Trudi's door, the door of the house they had, until recently, shared. Now, they were legally separated.

He knocked again. Trudi peered out an upstairs window and saw him there. She missed him and her heart was sore; they had been married nearly 35 years. But she was angry too: he was seeing someone else, a younger woman of course. It was a betrayal. She phoned her older brother Fred; he would tell her what to do.

"A separation means you stay separate," said Fred. "He wanted it, not you. Let him live with the consequences. Don't let him manipulate you."

"Trudi, please," said Leonard. "I know you're home." He knocked one more time. She trembled, waiting for him to leave, her hand on her heart, before descending the stairs to cook some supper. She never imagined her marriage could end like this.

Delores told the story, sitting in Belinda's living room with the cat-destroyed furniture, nearly 40 years after Leonard knocked on Trudi's door, but only a few hours after his funeral. "He didn't know what to do," concluded Delores; "he hadn't made up his mind."

Cousin Lorelei agreed. Trudi had confided in her during the period in question. "Why does he come to the bank where I work and just look at me across the room if he really wants a divorce?' she'd asked her niece.

The problem was, thought Belinda, he had loved both women. One was encouraging, easy to talk to, someone who explained what she needed and wanted. The other retained a certain glamour but she was difficult: she expected him to read her mind, and he still couldn't do it. He couldn't even get her to open the door, let alone figure out how to woo her all over again.

Yet Delores and Belinda could not help wondering: what if she had opened the door? What if they had reconciled? Would the same diseases have blighted their later lives in just the same way? Or would they have suffered even more without the devotion of new partners who wore themselves out in care-taking? It was impossible to know, but Belinda thought that Leonard's second marriage really had given him a second chance at happiness. For Trudi, though, the divorce was a catastrophe, producing both heartbreak and humiliation. The first simply had to be lived through; the second could only be reversed, in Trudi's view, by a second marriage.

Step-siblings

Belinda was an introvert. When she learned that her step-siblings would attend Leonard's funeral in Middleville, she was nervous. She had always liked Marjorie, coming all the way from Pennsylvania with her husband Ned, but had not seen her for 15 years, their last encounter at the funeral of Marjorie's mother (Belinda's stepmother) Grace. Grace had died of a cancer that progressed very fast, not long after Leonard was diagnosed with Alzheimer's disease. Marjorie had moved into the house to care for her mother, who soon became bed-ridden. What Belinda realized only in retrospect was that Marjorie had taken care of Leonard, too, bewildered by his wife's terrible illness. How does one re-pay such a debt?

Then there were Marjorie's older brother Max and his wife Tricia, whom Belinda had met only once before, virtual strangers who lived somewhere in Iowa. At least the funeral would give brother and sister an occasion to see each other. Perhaps it was not all about Leonard after all. Belinda simply did not know what to expect. She had not understood how well they knew him, but she learned her mistake by listening to their testimonies.

Marjorie spoke about him as a wit but not a snob: he welcomed everyone into his church choir, even the singers who needed help staying in tune. Tricia, a music teacher herself, noted what a tactful advisor he had been; and she and Max both described him as the perfect grandfatherly friend to their kids, one of whom (all grown up) attended the ceremony and nodded in agreement. All of these family members—were they her family members, too, Belinda now wondered?—talked about what a funny man Leonard had been. He had always been able to make them laugh.

Belinda understood that the fantasy of a Trudi-Leonard reconciliation, had it been realized, would have prevented the formation of her new, expanded family. But, really, this had been Leonard's family, and she was not sure she could lay claim to it. Geography and memory would separate them again.

Trudi's Second Marriage

After the divorce, Trudi had several boyfriends before she settled on Harry. One was rich and distinguished-looking; he offered her an expensive ring and wanted to make her his wife. But he was too old, she thought; she still felt young in her sixties and could not choose a man whose face and hair had become alike in silvery whiteness. She did not crave wealth but companionship—and the social status of being safely married to a vigorous man not likely to make her a widow any time soon.

Then there was the fellow who invited her on a road trip during which, he made clear, they would share the same motel room and the same bed. She refused, not about to leap into the sack with a man she barely knew. Indeed, she was insulted. By contrast, Harry's lack of sexual aggression was a selling point.

They met during the ballroom dancing lessons they both attended, the dance studio a hotbed of late-middle-age romance. Harry was a widower and a needy guy who freely admitted that he hated to be alone. He was Leonard's age, younger than Trudi and likely to last for a while. When she told him to give up smoking, he did. He was attentive, appreciative, and serious about her, and she felt suitably flattered. At first, she found it endearing that he wanted to be with her every minute. But, by the time she confessed to Delores that she felt "smothered" by him, they were already married, and she was stuck. For the next 20-some years, she would experience both gratitude for his attentions and resentment at having lost control of her life, sentiments intensified by the physical disabilities that may have been exacerbated by her felt loss of freedom in the first place.

Clearly, she had affection for him—and a certain grudging respect. She told Delores that, "having been in the military (during WWII),

Harry knew how to do things." And yet she felt frustrated, bored, and not desired. One day in the Lucky Stroke nursing home, Trudi astonished Belinda by complaining that Harry had never had sex with her in their entire marriage, "not even once!"

Belinda was not surprised by the facts of the case, as she remembered very well the time Harry had unselfconsciously explained that the beta blockers he took for his heart had rendered him impotent. Trudi had been annoyed with him for revealing such personal information, but Belinda and Delores had long suspected that the sex life of Trudi and Harry might have been limited to cuddling and kissing.

What surprised Belinda now was Trudi's vehemence on the matter, and she didn't know what to say, no doubt disgusting Trudi as an inadequate confidante. Inside her own mind, Belinda was awarding points to Leonard for his superior sexual prowess, but she knew that was silly. Poor Leonard could not even recognize Trudi now despite her many attempts to talk to him. Trudi told Delores that the man who looked like Leonard in the nursing home must be an "imposter," so little did he resemble the bright, witty man she used to know.

Trudi was reluctant to admit it, but her late-in-life relationships with men were shaped by disability: hers and theirs. Life, at the end, she thought, was altogether a disappointing business.

The Phone Call

It was November 9, 1981, Belinda's birthday. She was 32 years old. Young Ernest, at ten and a half months, strutted capably inside his playpen, sometimes grasping the rim and shaking it, as if he were a prisoner meditating an escape. It was evening, Belinda having taught two classes that day at the University of Maryland, her status in the academic hierarchy indicated by the location of her office in the sub-basement (the basement below the basement) of the English building.

Belinda thought it odd that no one from her family had sent her a birthday card, but people can be forgetful and the mail can be slow, so she was not unduly worried. Then the phone rang.

"I hate to tell you this on your birthday," began Trudi, "but your father and I are separated. He's seeing another woman. He got to know her when he gave her voice lessons. Now I think he wants a divorce."

Belinda was stunned. She knew her parents' marriage was not perfect, but perfect marriages did not exist. She thought it had been good enough to last. Perhaps Leonard was having some sort of mid-life crisis provoked by the move back to Pennsylvania, to take care of Lyle and Vicky, and the consequent collapse of his career. People in their 50's are not so attractive to employers as were the younger versions of themselves, but age discrimination came as a great shock to Leonard when it was applied to him. He would eventually cobble together an assortment of part-time jobs that kept him busy enough, but his earning power and professional status were sadly diminished.

These were the thoughts that came to Belinda later when she had recovered from the shock. But, on the phone, she could only feel sorry for Trudi, who was full of heartbreak and bitterness. She would never have predicted that her parents' marriage would come apart. Yet, putting the phone down, she was assailed by the rebellious idea that if they could get a divorce, she could too. She had no quarrel with Ernest Sr, who was kind, smart, and steadfast. Still, he was a husband, her husband, and had necessarily participated in helping to turn Belinda into a wife and a mother, roles with which she had increasingly come to feel at odds.

Part VII

Belinda Reflects

Safe at Home

Belinda was at a party. A woman, a new acquaintance, was telling the story of how she and her grown-up daughter had been terrified by a strange man knocking at their door one summer evening.

When the knock came, the woman had called out, "Who is it?" The man answered in an accent that marked him as an outsider to the community, not someone they recognized. The women froze in fear. The windows were open: he could climb in if he really wanted to. Finally, the daughter told the man to leave. After a few moments, he did. Then they called the cops.

Called the cops? The man had done nothing but knock on the door. When had this become suspicious behavior? Belinda said little: there was no point in arguing with existential dread. It's just that Belinda's own fears mostly took a different form.

Belinda knew that her own house was not at all secure. The doors to the house were half made of glass, old glass, not the new strong thick kind. Anyone with a rock and the willingness to use it could gain entrance. So far, in 23 years, no one had. It's true that there had been that drunken college student (or so Belinda imagined him to be), who had awakened her at 2 a.m. several years before by yanking at the front door knob. She had been asleep on the couch when the clamor gradually penetrated her consciousness. With some trepidation, she moved over to the door, saw a neatly dressed young man of college age, and yelled through the glass, "You don't live here! Go home!" Surely, he had recently left the downtown bars only a few blocks away and was drunk enough to be confused. Anyway, he left.

Belinda was only slightly more concerned when she discovered the broken storm panel on her bedroom window the next day. Next to it a small smear of blood suggested that, indeed, someone had tried

94

to climb in. Still employed at the time by the local university, she was too busy, she decided, to call the cops, so she e-mailed them about the incident when she reached her office. She didn't expect any specific action on their part; she just wanted to tell them about the doings in the neighborhood. They e-mailed back, tersely informing her that e-mail was no way to report an incipient crime. Belinda wondered whether such an episode would frighten her more now, given that she had more time to get nervous and worry about things.

She hoped not. Her fears had mostly not been about people outside her acquaintance, whom, admittedly, she generally avoided, but about the people she knew, who wished to penetrate her cocoon. Her house had always been her safe haven where no obnoxious committee member or student with a complaint could follow her. Even intimates were allowed only a certain amount of time before Belinda started to look yearningly toward the door. She was bad at sharing space with people; she knew it. But "space" wasn't really the right word. It was the emotional demands—of herself and others—that terrified her.

Burning the House Down

Most of the time, Belinda was boringly literal-minded. Fantasy fiction was her least favorite genre, and even in her own private fantasies, she demanded a semblance of realism. So, as she drank her morning coffee and paged through journal entries written fifteen months before, she was a bit surprised to re-encounter the following lines:

> Belinda had not burnt the house down on purpose. In fact, the claims adjustor maintained that her failure to turn off her electric tea kettle had probably not contributed to the blaze at all. Faulty wiring and tinder-dry weather had done the damage. Nonetheless, Belinda worried that she was responsible: the one day on which she had left the kettle on was the same day on which her house went up in flames. She got back from the nursing home just in time to save her cats from dying of smoke inhalation, but not in time to save the kitchen and dining room from being demolished or to keep her books from stinking of smoke forever.
>
> The house was a total loss—too old and rickety to begin with to be worth rebuilding— so Belinda and the cats were effectively homeless. She tried not to reveal her exhilaration at the news. After all, it wasn't as if she could just pick up and leave Middleville. Her parents were still in the nursing home, and she couldn't just dump the cats at the pound. Still. She felt so much lighter! Tons of things nailing her to the spot had suddenly been removed, and she felt free.

In real life, Belinda had never been a fire starter at all, although it was true that she sometimes forgot to turn off her heat-producing appliances. However, she did remember that the fire fantasy was not entirely new. She had mostly enjoyed her job at Middleville State, but in the bad years when she had not, she had sometimes imagined a campus blaze, ignited not by herself, but by some merciful god as an act of deliverance, because, of course, she could not just quit.

This memory caused her to ask herself what had been going on fifteen months before, from which she might have been pining for deliverance. Her journal made that clear too: Trudi was trying to die, and Belinda was trying to stop her, often retreating into denial, apparently to avoid thinking about what was really happening.

Now that Trudi and Leonard were both gone, Belinda mourned their loss, but no longer wished to burn down her house. Instead, she was having it painted by careful workers who conscientiously scraped away many old decaying fragments before applying a pristine layer of new, fresh paint.

Dinner at the Lucky Stroke

It was noon on a rainy Sunday, and Belinda felt at a loss. A few months ago, she would have been at the Lucky Stroke nursing home feeding Leonard and wondering whether she was doing him an injustice in helping to keep him alive.

Still, there had been pleasures afforded by such a routine. Belinda enjoyed the conversation of Ruby, for example, who was the responsible mother of two young daughters but who still liked to reminisce about her childhood years as a hellion. She and her older brother had, more than once, tossed their younger brother into the dryer, albeit only for a few seconds: fortunately, he was still alive and relatively unscathed. Ruby was, of course, much too vigilant to allow any such shenanigans at her house now. She was also a skilled aide who excelled in getting people fed, seeming to have a magical ability to encourage effective chewing and swallowing.

Then there was Ladue, a 40-year veteran of nursing-home work but still too young to retire. Somehow, she had not been ground down by the system, and Belinda was always calmed by her quiet competence. Ladue liked to talk about her fiancé, who had been her fiancé for 20 years because, having tried marriage in her youth, she decided that it was not for her. Oh, it's true that she had gotten some lovely children out of the deal, and they had already made her a grandmother (and soon-to-be great-grandmother). But she would never marry again. She and her fiancé loved each other just fine and probably always would, without benefit of clergy.

Belinda missed these women, having already begun to do so even while Leonard was still alive. They had been reassigned to other dining room tables and were replaced by very young women who gave Belinda pitying looks, as if to say, "You won't be doing this very much longer."

The Secret Past

"Keep the past secret," said a recent horoscope column directed at Scorpios. The idea was not to allow one's public life to be contaminated or compromised by one's secret sins or inevitable mistakes or by the scandals of one's family. Belinda remembered being told by her parents when she was a child that it was not the thing to do to tell all and sundry that her German grandfather had died in a mental institution. This fact was *personal*, not to be shared, whereas she had regarded it as fascinating and exotic, something special to talk about. She was, perhaps, too young to understand that mental illness carried a stigma—that the whole family could be adversely branded if the wrong people heard about Fritz. Lots of families kept the past secret back then—and the present, too, if it was likely to disgrace them. But, surely, such advice was outmoded now that people wrote memoirs telling tales which made even experienced readers like Belinda flinch.

The fact is that Belinda had been constructing—and sometimes resurrecting—monuments to the past for a few months now. She had had the wedding portrait of Trudi and Leonard expertly framed, the winsome couple now gracing a place of honor on her dining room wall. Of course, a wedding photo is simply an artifact of an event already part of the public record. What about all those stories she had been telling about the dead, portraying them not at their best but at (what she regarded as) their most human?

Trudi would have been mortified had she known what Belinda would do, she who had been relatively tight-lipped about (or maybe just ignorant of) her family's history. But Leonard would have had to see that Belinda's story-telling was an extension of his—that she was making use of stories she had complained about hearing from him in the first place.

Belinda did not believe, for a moment, that there was a Trudi or Leonard consciousness in the universe who could upbraid her now. Nonetheless, she hoped that they would not feel betrayed by her were they to come back to life. She feared that Trudi would. But they would not come back to life—except in the stories and memories of the living—and so she could not (just yet) let them go.

The Movies

In the 1950's, when Belinda was a child, American parents did not hover over their offspring. Small children walked to school by themselves, or with other small children, in what appeared to be, and usually was, perfect safety. On one such walk, when Belinda was probably six, if not younger, a small boy of similar age took her in his arms and kissed her. Undoubtedly, he was re-enacting a scene from a Hollywood movie he had watched, possibly from a backseat perch at a drive-in.

Belinda was thrilled. There was nothing in the least off-putting about the kiss. There was no slimy saliva, no sexual undertones (not that she would have been able to identify them anyway), no fear-inducing desire. It was pure play-acting, and Belinda felt swept up in the drama. Her only source of discontent was that she never saw the little boy, or experienced that particular thrill, again.

Still, as an avid movie-watcher herself, Belinda had to wonder whether her addiction to the cinema had distorted her entire view of life and art. Had she persistently misread *Wuthering Heights* because she couldn't get Olivier's portrayal of Heathcliff out of her head? Did Hemingway's self-absorbed characters, Lady Brett and Jake Barnes, become tragic figures in the movie version only because Ava Gardner and Tyrone Power were so gorgeous and sexy? (Belinda remembered watching that film before she had learned the definition of the classic war wound and, therefore, before she could understand exactly what their romantic problem was.)

But it wasn't just that the movies glamourized classic novels; they glamourized life. An important feminist movie theorist had, long ago, complained that golden age Hollywood films promoted misogyny by portraying women as beautiful objects and dangerous *femmes fatales*.

Belinda did not disagree. She would even admit that such portrayals had not entirely disappeared. However, that was not the problem that bothered her. The problem for her, she thought, was that the movies she wanted to watch glorified *all* the possibilities too much. Yet she was pining for the movie version of her life because there always *were* possibilities for the movie heroine, who would not be reduced to gazing out the window and counting the stars. She was an aging dreamer, nourished on old movies and even older books, confronting a new century that she could bear to look at only through her own ironic lens.

The Ingenue

Belinda was vain about her looks. Not that she imagined she was pretty. Rather, she imagined that she looked young. Not to the truly young, of course, who could spot a senior citizen anywhere—and reliably give her the appropriate discount at the movies without her even asking. No, it was the middle-aged people already old enough to be insecure about their own looks who professed to be shocked when they discovered her advanced age.

Belinda enjoyed "shocking" people in this way, knowing that both of her parents had liked playing this game as well. Alzheimer's had forced Leonard to give it up, perhaps prematurely, for the middle-aged nurse at the hospital had opined that he was a handsome man just a few weeks before his death. Trudi, for her part, was famous at the nursing home for putting on make-up almost until the end. When she looked in the mirror and lamented, "Who would want me now?," Belinda should have known that the end was near.

Still, Belinda tried to explain to people that her genetic inheritance of smooth skin (Was that all it boiled down to? That and her dyed hair?) did not seem to correlate to any more useful characteristics. To the contrary, it allowed her to imagine herself as the *ingenue*— an innocent young female creature, said the dictionary, or a person *playing* such a role—all too long. Indeed, it seemed to Belinda that she had been playing the ingenue all her life. The longevity of her parents had helped her to maintain this fiction. When she sang to Leonard in the nursing home dining room, people would say, "Oh, there's that girl singing to her father."

Now there were no parents left in comparison to whom Belinda could feel young, no parents to refer to Belinda and Delores as "the girls." She wondered whether she would move directly from not being taken seriously because she was young and female (the ingenue) to not being taken seriously because she was old and female (the old lady). She wondered whether she wished to be taken seriously. Maybe it was a source of freedom not to be.

Jack Benny

When Belinda was a child, a comedian named Jack Benny had a TV show which revolved around a couple of major conceits endlessly repeated and exploited. One was that he could play the violin, which he did only briefly and only to show that he had mastered the knack of playing comically badly. The other was that he would remain aged 39 forever, despite all evidence to the contrary, which included massive eye-rolling on his part and the skepticism of his black manservant Rochester, a sort of Stepin Fetchit character whose portrayal would be considered racist today. (It was. Nevertheless, he was also a descendant of Shakespeare's fools, who told the truth when no one else would.)

The thing is that Jack Benny told people when youth ended: at 40, so don't admit to it. But that cultural consensus had shifted, thought Belinda, so that people were no longer sure when youth was over and old age began.

When Belinda was about to turn 40, she asked a friend to throw a party for her, to which she wore a black dress, but, really, she had not been in mourning. In retrospect, she thought, she had been in her prime, and old photos suggested as much.

Soon, though, she would turn 70, a much scarier number. She remembered how both her parents had grown old rather suddenly in their 70's, Leonard exhibiting symptoms of Alzheimer's disease and Trudi having undiagnosed strokes that increasingly disabled her, their long-enduring youth swiftly wiped out.

Still, she would have a party. It seemed as if she spent her days planning public events that memorialized her private mortality: the funerals of her parents came to mind. But what else could she do?

106

Pretend to be 39 forever? She would confess her age. She would celebrate the past 70 years—and hope that she got a few more good ones.

Part VIII

Epilogue

Cult Classic

Belinda was 70. She felt a girl still, but an old woman too. Would her mental abilities begin to dwindle noticeably, as Leonard's had, by the age of 75? Would she have strokes like Trudi? No one had been able to protect them from their fates. No one could protect Belinda from hers either. Everyone does studies in mortality, the one course no one can escape, and Belinda understood that the deaths of her parents were just the introduction. She had many more chapters ahead of her. But, meanwhile, she felt the surge of her own living power to call the images of the elders back into the world, to celebrate the legacies they had left her, and then to tell her own story as she knew it thus far, the story they had given her, but also the building she must do upon it, creating her own plot until her powers failed.

It did not matter that she was not Elizabeth Bennet or Jane Eyre. Titillated by the whispers of ancestors who had given her life, Belinda felt that the inevitable finitude all mortals shared was not her only inheritance from them, but that Lotte's grit, Trudi's resilience, and Leonard's idealism (itself nurtured by his elders' hopes) remained the more distinctive legacy. Their work—their sacrifices—had allowed her to become the woman who was not defined by the romantic other or the needs of the young, but who was able to take a different path on a journey she was just beginning to describe. She wanted to create a cult classic, an edgy tale that would dispense with the plots of the past, even as she honored the forebears who had lived by them.

Acknowledgments

It is a truism that writers are influenced by nearly every word they have ever read or heard, but here I want to acknowledge a couple of explicit references consciously used. I adopt the name "Brewer" for my fictionalized version of Reading, Pennsylvania, because that is what John Updike called it in his Rabbit novels. When I cite the *Brewer Times* obituary of Dr. Isaac Reinherz, I am, in actuality, quoting the *Reading Times* article that appeared on 29 June 1945, reporting the death of Dr. A. N. Seidel (a page-one story).

I am also indebted to the exciting new play by Matthew Lopez, *The Inheritance* (2018), for causing me to regard my family's collective memories and stories as legacies, a kind of inheritance exploited and treasured by the Belinda character in these vignettes. More tangible legacies include the photographs I describe and the painting of peonies by my grandfather's cousin, Elda Craumer: I am sorry I never knew her, for I am grateful for her work. I am also grateful to Mary Pipher for suggesting, in *Women Rowing North* (2019), that older women can write their own plots and take control of their own stories.

I will forever be in the debt of all the Facebook readers who commented on my Belinda posts, asking questions, offering encouragement, and helping me to understand what worked and what did not. I am especially lucky to have had the help of two fine editors, Betsy Delmonico (of Golden Antelope Press) and Joanna B. Marshall, who gently imposed order on Belinda's chaos, suggested needed connections I had not yet made, and guided me to the points that required further development. (Any remaining flaws are mine alone!) Joanna also took the photo of the painting that graces the cover, and Betsy sketched out the family tree that it had not occurred to me to create. Robert L. Costic provided much-needed computer advice and assistance.

As much of Belinda's drama occurs in the nursing home where her parents lived out their final years, I would like to thank all of the staff members who worked at the LaPlata Nursing Home in LaPlata, Missouri, between 2013 and 2019, for all their assistance and support. Among the members of this group, a number of people stand out: Donna Cook, Angie Capps, Tracy Thompson, Mary Moore, Jenny Littlefield, Jade Hughes, and Candi Cole. All of these women helped me and my parents greatly, and I quote or paraphrase most of them. I am more thankful than I can say to my sister Deb Seidel for her wisdom and patience—and her willingness to share the stories I did not know. In addition, my cousin Rose-Marie Rose turned out to be a wonderfully reliable reader and information source. Of course, my greatest debt is to my elders, whose stories I have appropriated and who might feel, alternately, outraged and honored on every page, were they alive to read me.